SARAH TOMCZAK

is the author of *The Good Date Guide* and has spent the last ten years writing for women's magazines in New York and London. She was a lifestyle editor at *Us Weekly* and has written on style and sex for *Cosmopolitan, Company, Closer, Top Sante,* and YM *Magazine*.

How to Live Like a Lady

LESSONS IN LIFE, MANNERS, AND STYLE

Sarah Tomczak

THE LYONS PRESS

An imprint of The Globe Pequot Press

Guilford, Connecticut

Copyright © 2007 by Elwin Street Limited
First Lyons Press edition, 2008

Conceived and produced by
Elwin Street Limited
144 Liverpool Road
London N1 1LA

10 9 8 7 6

Designed by Jon Wainwright, Alchemedia Design
Illustrated by Micca/Dutch Uncle
Picture credits: The Advertising Archives p92; The Bridgeman Art Library p110
While every effort has been made to acknowledge copyright holders, Elwin Street Limited
would like to apologize for any omissions.

Printed in China

ISBN 978-1-59921-352-1

Library of Congress Cataloging-in-Publication data is available on file.

CONTENTS

Foreword
BY DIANA MATHER

A couple of years ago I was asked by friends if there were courses to help give their daughters confidence and a bit of polish, and I realized that most of the established finishing schools had closed down. I started to research why these schools were no longer popular. Girls today still want to know how to behave appropriately in any situation, but they don't want to spend a year doing it. Older women from their twenties to their fifties sometimes feel that there is a gap in their knowledge as far as etiquette, protocol, and manners are concerned, and from this The Public Image School of Etiquette was born. Our five-day courses give people a broad look at life skills as well as learning how to walk with poise or how to hold a knife and fork properly.

I was very pleased to be asked to write the foreword for this book as I believe it is very important to put emphasis on modern manners and ladylike behavior—part of my mission is to do just that.

Being a lady means different things to different people. To me, it means treating other people with kindness and consideration, and if possible keeping your cool and acting with decorum at all times—in short, having good manners. Being a lady also means celebrating your femininity.

Confidence and self-belief are two of the greatest gifts you can give anybody and part of that confidence comes from knowing the rules; if you know the rules you can decide whether or not to keep them. Etiquette evolves over time, and so a book such as this is extremely valuable as it gives advice and tips on twenty-first-century etiquette and conduct, in an un-stuffy, fun, and lively way. It is essential to keep up with the trends in acceptable behavior and this book will help you do just that—it is also great fun!

The Public Image School of Etiquette Top Ten Tips

1. Always smile when you meet someone.
2. Say "How do you do" or "Hello"
   not "Pleased to meet you" when greeting.
3. Don't kiss on the first meeting.
4. Stand up when others enter the room.
5. Don't use cell phones during mealtimes or text in company.
6. Don't leave the table during a meal—if you're desperate to visit the bathroom, wait until after the dessert.
7. Drink a glass of water to match every glass of wine. Don't get drunk!
8. Mind your Ps and Qs. Always write to say thank you after dinner, a weekend stay, a present, etc.
9. Dress appropriately—don't show too much cleavage or leg at formal events.
10. If in doubt about anything—wines, food, dress, or etiquette—ask!

INTRODUCTION

It's not easy to remain ladylike when those around you are getting lazier by the minute. Many women have given up altogether. Their defection means that flashing too much flesh and sharing their bodily functions with the world has become so commonplace that exercising good manners now seems positively old-fashioned.

But it doesn't have to be this way! Social graces not only make the world a much more pleasant place, but they make you a much more pleasant person. Behaving like a lady can ensure you a place on every party guest list, make you the most popular girl in the office, and yes, even help you procure the man of your dreams.

However, many of the old rules no longer apply. It's not necessary to let a man order for you in a restaurant and it's become de rigueur to air-kiss your friends when greeting them. Sending a text message is now a perfectly acceptable way to invite a friend for dinner and you no longer have to home-cook every course you serve up. With our fast-paced lives and the never-ending advancement of modern communication, only the most conscientious of ladies can be bothered to switch off her cell phone, turn down her iPod, avoid hitting "reply all" on her e-mail, and get out her pen and paper to send a thank-you note.

So how do you navigate your way through this modern minefield and avoid social faux pas?

That's where this chic little manual comes in handy. The following six chapters contain everything you need to know about behaving like a lady in today's society. You'll develop the art of elegant speech, learn how to introduce yourself and make small talk, how to avoid conversational blunders, and how to hold an engaging conversation with anyone.

You'll learn how to use your body language to your advantage, how to stand with poise, how to sit like a lady, and the secret to walking gracefully, even in towering heels. You may think that getting out of a car is easy, but doing it with style is a little more complicated. You only have to look at the unfortunate pictures in the papers of celebrities exposing their underwear to see that this must be a subtle art!

There's an entire section on style and good grooming, because there's no bigger calamity than wearing an inappropriate outfit to a soirée or revealing a visible panty line to disapproving companions. Image is, of course, essential to every lady, and although natural style cannot be taught, dressing to suit your figure and wearing the right outfit for every occasion can.

And though there's no denying Audrey Hepburn is the epitome of elegance, it took Eliza Dolittle more than a new outfit to become a Fair Lady, so once we have learned how to be chic, we move on to learning how to be a fabulous guest, as well as what to wear, how to behave, and what to bring to various parties to which you may receive an invite. The dinner table is a potential etiquette nightmare, so there is a helpful section on cracking the code with tips on how to tackle particularly tricky food—before you bought this book, your bungled attempts to dismantle these foods could well have left your dinner companions open mouthed! And what about when you are the hostess? Look no further and no longer fear the ring of the door bell—we look at perfect party preparation to ensure that an invite to your place will be the hottest ticket in town.

You'll then learn the importance of maintaining your ladylike ways when out in society; it is crucial that you present the best version of you when traveling from A to B, when on the search for Mr. Right, and when dealing with modern communication.

Finally you'll learn the secrets of the successful job interview, ladylike office etiquette, how to treat colleagues cordially, and how to get ahead in business, as well as the secret to never making a cultural slip-up abroad.

Being a lady is a full-time job—you'll always need stamps in your purse, a stock of thank-you cards at hand, and your favorite florist on speed-dial. You'll always have to be generous of spirit and humble of character. You may never take the last slice of cake or be the most drunk person at a party; you simply cannot boast about your pay raise or reveal the saucy details of your sex life. Snobbery is all around us, and while as a lady you must learn to tolerate the slip-ups of others, there's no certainty that the same good grace will be afforded you.

Grace, poise, generosity, elegance, vivacity, wisdom, and wit—wouldn't it be just lovely to possess all of these ladylike qualities? And now you can with this thoroughly modern and stylishly savvy guide to etiquette. Read on for everything you need to know about being a modern lady.

CHAPTER
1

TALK THE TALK

In this chapter, you'll learn:

✦ How to make a good first impression ✦ How to introduce others
✦ The rules of the greeting kiss ✦ How to make scintillating small talk
✦ How to listen well ✦ The art of good conversation

What you say matters

As children we were always prompted to "say thank you for having me to stay," to "say please," and "ask nicely." Even now as adults, remembering to speak properly and politely is essential for every lady but it doesn't always come naturally. While appearances are certainly vital, it's your speech that reveals your inner beauty. What you say, how you say it, and the effect of your words on those around you are the truest measure of your sophistication. And sometimes it takes practice.

Have you ever listened to a recording of yourself and wanted to deny vehemently that the voice even belongs to you? Accents sound broader, words more mumbled, and sentences not nearly as eloquent as you had intended at the time. While gabbing on the phone to a girlfriend offers the opportunity for a good old gossip and stream-of-consciousness chatter, your aim in other social situations is for well-thought-out, concise, and charming conversation. Others will delight to talk with you and inevitably you will enjoy the conversations more.

Throughout this chapter you'll learn how to make an instant good impression, the art of great conversation, and how to cope with any verbal faux pas (because no one's immune to a slip of the tongue from time to time!). No matter how broad your dialect or how spicy your conversation, the most essential lesson you'll learn is that you should make whomever you are talking with feel at ease—from the big-business boss to your elderly neighbor whose backyard flora you've just been admiring. Put others at ease, and happy and interesting conversations will flow freely.

Smooth introductions

Pain-free introductions begin with a smile, an appropriate word of formality, and move quickly to a relaxed conversation topic that interests both parties. It's not a science; it's an art. Practise these pointers and you'll master it in no time.

Smiles are free!

Before you even utter a greeting, the first thing to remember is that a good mood is infectious. Earn a reputation for always having a smile on your face and a sunny disposition. Forget your aches and pains, the answer to "How are you?" is always "Fine, thank you." Unless you're talking with your nearest and dearest, nobody wants to hear about the latest argument with your boyfriend or that you've spent over your credit limit again. Get yourself onto every guest list in town by being such a bright, breezy person that you exude cheerfulness. Who doesn't want a friend like that? When you see someone you know on the street, greet them with a genuine smile, look them in the eye to create an instant bond, and offer an enthusiastic, "Hello! How lovely to bump into you."

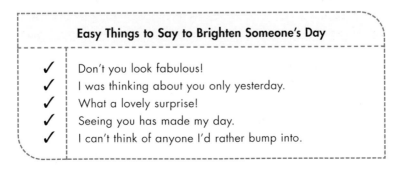

Easy Things to Say to Brighten Someone's Day

- ✓ Don't you look fabulous!
- ✓ I was thinking about you only yesterday.
- ✓ What a lovely surprise!
- ✓ Seeing you has made my day.
- ✓ I can't think of anyone I'd rather bump into.

Is FORMAL too FORMAL?

The simple answer is no. When you're introducing yourself to someone for the first time, always take the formal route, and call them by their title and surname, for example "Mrs. Jones," until they suggest otherwise. In this day and age, a casual approach is most common and you probably won't be expected to address someone so formally for long, but the older generations do appreciate it, and would rather invite you to call them by their first name than have you assume from the start that it's acceptable. This is especially true in America and in Europe, where anyone who is your senior in age or authority should be referred to as Mr., Mrs., or any other appropriate title, such as Professor or Doctor.

MAKING the FIRST move

Now we have that cleared up, on to the introduction itself. There's nothing wrong with being a little bold and introducing yourself first. With that winning smile again, introduce yourself using your name, and when they give theirs, use it straight away in conversation: "Mrs. Jones, it's such a pleasure to meet you." Saying someone's name out loud as soon as you've heard it is a great trick to help you remember it in the future. Try to ingrain that name into your memory to avoid hiccups down the line.

OOPS! I FORGOT their NAME!

First rule: Don't panic. Getting more flustered never helps. If you can, casually and discretely ask a third person nearby to remind you of the name you've forgotten, or take the bold route and come clean by saying, "I am terribly sorry, but I've managed to forget your name." You're not the first person in the world to have drawn a blank and it's far better to ask for a memory jog than to dwell on it for too long—or worse, allow the conversation go on for minutes while you are searching your memory banks for the person's name. The situation can become excruciating if you then need to introduce another friend to this person whose name you've quite forgotten. The best idea is to ask for the reminder at the outset to avoid further embarrassment.

Likewise, don't let anyone stew if they seem to have forgotten your name or called you by the wrong one. Correct them the first time they get your name wrong rather than letting them repeat it. Make light of it by saying, "Actually, it's Katherine. Don't worry, I'm terrible with names too!" Admitting you often make mistakes with names will quickly put the other person at ease. Remember, it's all about making the person you are speaking with feel relaxed in your presence.

HOW TO INTRODUCE OTHERS

While being friends with a social butterfly takes the pressure off you, introducing yourself to new people can be easier than standing alongside, waiting for your big moment. Wait until there's a natural break in conversation before interjecting with, "Hello, we haven't met before. I'm Katherine and I know [the host] from work/yoga/college."

If you have brought guests along it's your responsibility to introduce them to others. Create an icebreaker by mentioning something they have in common, such as "This is Sally, who also works in advertising." After highlighting their shared interest, you can slip off and do a little mingling of your own.

To KISS or NOT to KISS?

Faced with the dilemma of whether or not a kiss on the cheek when greeting someone is appropriate, it's important to read your audience. In many countries a kiss can be a social greeting that is certainly not reserved just for your nearest and dearest. On page 19 is a quick guide to how many kisses are expected in different countries.

To avoid leaving unsightly lipstick marks on another person's cheek, press your cheek, instead of your lips, against theirs and kiss the air beside their face. If you happen to bump foreheads midway, just laugh it off as an icebreaker and make a mental note for next time.

Reserved Brits and Germans are often more comfortable shaking hands; in this case, offer your hand before the person you're greeting has a chance to lean in for a kiss, to save embarrassment. Make your handshake firm, but not bone crunching, and look the person in the eye and smile at the same time. Friends' parents, prospective employers, and older people should be greeted with a handshake, as a general rule. Hugs should only be proffered to true pals; though if you're greeting a group of both friends and acquaintances, save time and some awkward space-invading by sticking to handshakes or pecks all round.

One last note on kissing: keep it sweet. Your breath, that is. Store a stash of mints in your handbag, so you can freshen up before an introduction, because no one wants to get too intimate with a clove of garlic.

How Many Kisses?

United States	One or two kisses.
United Kingdom	One or two for family and close friends. Stick to the handshake for the safe option.
Canada	One or two.
Australia and New Zealand	One or none.
France	Three or sometimes four kisses, always beginning on the left cheek.
Netherlands	Three kisses. If you are greeting an elderly or close member of the family, add a few more to show your affection, always ending with the cheek you started with.
Germany	One or two for close family or friends, but handshakes are the norm. Sometimes friends will shake hands and kiss at the same time.
Italy	Hugs and handshakes predominate rather than kisses, which are restricted to very close friends.
Spain	Two kisses; strictly right cheek first.
Scandinavia	Two kisses.
Russia	Three kisses.

THE DELICATE ART OF GOOD CONVERSATION

Once the introductions are out of the way, the next skill you need in your repertoire is polished conversation. Possibly the worst thing you could be is a bore (who'd want to be stuck with you at a party?), so it's imperative to learn how to chat with people of all backgrounds and ages. The secret to your success is to discover something in which the other person is interested and to show a fascination in it yourself.

Use the small amount of knowledge you have about a person. Do they know the host from work? Do they still have a tan from a recent holiday? Have you bumped into them at any events before? Ask questions, show genuine interest in the other person, and let the conversation grow organically from their answers. Your aim is to find topics of common interest, to strike upon something the other person loves to talk about and which genuinely interests you as well. Your astute questioning will lead to scintillating conversation and the person you're talking with will find you charming. Mindless chatter is easy enough to pull off, but having a truly absorbing, enriching conversation can be the difference between a good night and a great night. So think hard about what would make an interesting dialogue and hunt for that common ground.

STOP, LOOK, LISTEN

Listening is just as important a skill to develop as talking—most people are delighted to be able to chat about themselves or their recent exploits. Take a tip from hairdressers, for whom an ability to small-talk is just as essential as their prowess with the scissors. Ask about jobs,

Great Small-talk Subjects

✓ Favorite places to vacation.
✓ Human-interest stories from the newspapers.
✓ Sports.
✓ The latest must-see TV.
✓ Weird and wonderful diet tips.
✓ Classic bands and cult albums.
✓ The weekend weather.
✓ Local neighborhoods and new shops that have opened.

vacations, weekend plans, and favorite places to shop. Avoid personal questions, relationships, politics, and especially money—always an absolute no-no. Remember that the essence of great conversation is to be inclusive, so ask questions that anyone would feel happy answering. If you do run out of things to say, inject a little new life into your conversation by widening the group of people you are talking to.

Part of being a good listener also includes the way you respond to what people say. Be sympathetic and don't offer controversial or negative opinions—at least before you know the other person better. A juicy argument never makes for a warm and fuzzy atmosphere and people rarely look for sage advice from a stranger.

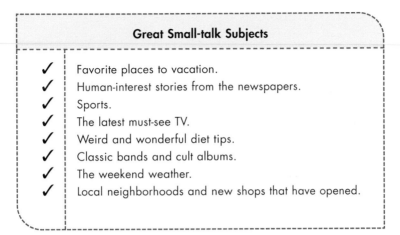

THE **THINGS** YOU **SHOULD** TRY **NOT** TO **SAY**

It's sometimes difficult, but try to practice discretion and tact at all times. Most of the sins of bad conversation come from talking too much rather than too little, so think before you speak, as you cannot take back anything you say under the glare of the spotlight. And no matter how juicy that tidbit you just heard is, keep it to yourself. Save any gossiping for private conversations with only your very closest.

Humor is a great social lubricant and if you've got a well-honed sense of humor you'll be the life of the party. But stick to being self-deprecating and resist the urge to turn your sharp tongue on others—there's nothing worse than being perceived as bitchy or malicious, especially when you're really attempting to be dry and witty.

Don't try to bowl people over with your academic brilliance either. Make your audience feel inadequate and you're guaranteed to fall out of favor faster than you can recite the periodic table.

Avoid insincerity. No one likes a faker, so only show enthusiasm if you really mean it. The same goes for empty promises. If you insist "We must meet for dinner soon," follow up with a phone call or e-mail a few days later to show that you are still keen to get together.

Finally, remember that silence can be golden. It is not necessary to fill every gap in conversation with mindless chatter. And it's fine to take a back seat sometimes and be a great listener instead of a glittering entertainer.

How to climb out of the hole you've just dug for yourself

How do you handle those awkward silences, when you realize you've uttered the wrong thing? If you asked about a boyfriend or girlfriend, unaware of a break-up, offer a brief, sincere apology and change the subject quickly. If you hadn't known already that the relationship was over, you're probably not close enough to discuss the intimate details anyway.

If you fear you may unwittingly have offended someone, first assess the damage. You don't want to dig yourself deeper into that hole with justifications or effusive apologies, so a swift change of subject could be in order. However, if your companion is boiling with rage, there's no way around it—apologize, before moving on to a less controversial subject. Fill any awkward silences with harmless questions or observations from which you can start up a new line of conversation.

How to speak properly

Your delivery is, of course, just as important as your message. Speaking well is like writing a letter on your fanciest notepaper—the words always sound better and will please the recipient or listener. Luckily, times have changed since everyone was expected to speak with exactly the same accent, and now regional accents are better appreciated. Just make sure your accent is decipherable to the listener and avoid using colloquial terms for the interim if it will help make yourself understood.

Listen to yourself

Think about how many hours we spend primping and preening in a mirror, yet we hardly put any energy into the way we sound, compared to the way we look. For a sneak peek into what everyone else hears, try listening to your answer-phone message. Do you mumble or gabble your words too quickly? Think about the language you use too: Do you have any annoying words or catchphrases that you overuse without even meaning to? Do you overuse "filler" words such as "like" or "really"? Swearing is pretty gross, but then again so is bad grammar, and a lady should do her best to avoid both.

Think about the volume of your voice too—no matter how compelling your conversation, your companion won't appreciate being blasted, and others in the room don't need to hear your every word, so keep your voice down.

A vast vocabulary is a bonus but not essential. Creating a good impression doesn't require cramming your speech with flowery words and if it's possible to say something in five words rather than fifteen, do so.

Personal space

Consider how close you stand when you're talking with someone you've just met at a function. You know there's nothing worse than feeling your personal space invaded by another, so think about your approach. If you can feel their breath on your cheek, you're standing too close! If your companion keeps inching back a step, you're crowding them in. An arm's length is a comfortable distance apart for most people—anything drastically private you have to say to one another that might require whispering should be saved for a later date.

Ten Things You Should Never Do During Polite Conversation

1. Speak so loudly that the entire party can hear your every word.
2. Stand so close you know what brand of deodorant someone uses.
3. Boast about your bank balance or boyfriend's virility.
4. Swear like a trooper.
5. Share your medical and emotional ailments.
6. Whisper your deepest darkest, secrets.
7. Talk about yourself too much . . .
8. Or gossip about everyone else.
9. Laugh too uproariously.
10. Yawn.

WHAT TO DO WHEN YOU BLOW YOUR TOP

OK, there might just be some occasions when your elegant façade slips slightly. But blowing your top and launching into a tirade of abuse when things aren't going your way is a surefire way to shatter your reputation. Whether you are complaining to a shop assistant about a faulty pair of shoes or confronting a colleague about a work issue, keep a clear head and try to remain composed. Offer solutions to a problem and be as accommodating as you can without compromising too much. If you become really incensed, instead of flying off the handle, take a physical step back, out of the confrontation, and count to ten before you utter another word.

Stop your blood boiling by trying this breathing trick: instead of sucking in your stomach when you breathe in and relaxing it when you breathe out, switch it around, so that you push your tummy out as you inhale, then suck it in as you exhale. It's tricky to get the hang of, but concentrating on this instead of the situation instantly switches your attention, and a bit of deep breathing gives you the chance to calm down and clear your head.

If you know a stressful situation lies ahead, try dabbing lavender essential oil on either wrist beforehand and sniff your wrist the moment you feel yourself getting worked up, in order to benefit from its calming effect.

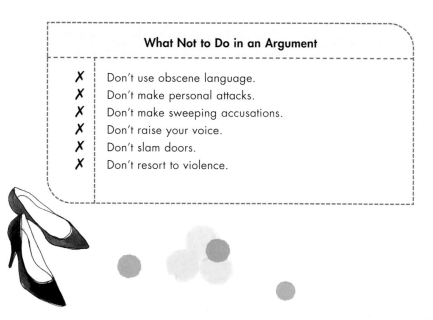

What Not to Do in an Argument

✗ Don't use obscene language.
✗ Don't make personal attacks.
✗ Don't make sweeping accusations.
✗ Don't raise your voice.
✗ Don't slam doors.
✗ Don't resort to violence.

HOW TO REACT TO RUDE PEOPLE

Judge every incident before reacting—instead of rising to a rude remark, diffuse the situation with a smile and say, "Oh, that's not a very polite thing to say!" If asked an offensive question, try saying, "I don't think I feel like answering that" while also smiling. The tone of your voice can be light, and your smile will show you are refusing to feel offended, yet your words make it clear that this is a conversation you are not prepared to have.

If you cannot clear the air without becoming angrier in the process, ask if you can continue the discussion at a later date once you have had a chance to calm down. You don't want to say something in the heat of the moment that you could later regret.

HOW TO ACCEPT A COMPLIMENT . . .

It's funny that we sometimes find it easier to deal with an insult than to accept a compliment. Don't be bashful or embarrassed and don't negate the flattery by denying it or causing too much of a fuss. Next time someone pays you a compliment, just smile and say a genuine thank you.

Resist the urge to divulge too much unnecessary information, which only draws the moment out. If someone admires your dress, don't tell them where you bought it and exactly how much you paid. You don't need to tell the world all your secrets. French women know that an air of mystery, a certain je ne sais quoi, is a healthy thing. It's safe to say that they wouldn't be revealing that their silk scarf was actually discovered at the bottom of a bargain bin. And don't forget to add a dose of humility—while accepting a compliment gracefully is appropriate, agreeing with it wholeheartedly is most certainly not.

. . . And HOW to BESTOW ONE

It's such a super confidence boost to receive a compliment, so don't be shy about handing them out either. Mention anything that impresses you enough to comment on, from the surroundings, the cocktails, or the abundance of guests, to the hostess's fabulous shoes. Everyone likes to know they're doing something right and this is the best way to make the person you're talking to feel good.

The ability to give comments well is an art form—too many and you seem insincere, so be careful to bestow them only when you really mean what you say. An old-fashioned rule of thumb was that men love to be complimented on their conversation and women on their closet. But times have changed and many men would now be delighted to be complimented on their attire, while many women care more how you judge their professional and social achievements over the cut of their frock. If you do coo over a fabulous handbag, just remember that asking where it was purchased can be a delicate matter (most woman like to keep their little-known boutiques under wraps) and asking how much it cost is always a total no-no.

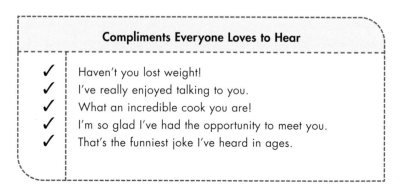

Compliments Everyone Loves to Hear

✓ Haven't you lost weight!
✓ I've really enjoyed talking to you.
✓ What an incredible cook you are!
✓ I'm so glad I've had the opportunity to meet you.
✓ That's the funniest joke I've heard in ages.

LAUGHING AND SHOUTING

Laughing at someone's joke may be the ultimate compliment you can pay them, but not if yours is a guffaw rather than a giggle. At finishing schools ladies are taught to laugh on a musical scale. It doesn't matter if yours is not as melodic, just make sure you don't shriek, bray, or cackle, and that you aren't risking anyone's eardrums the moment you erupt into laughter.

There are certain times and places for humor—a play, a business seminar, or a religious service are definitely not places to get the giggles, so if there's ever been a time to exercise composure, do it now.

Shouting is perfect at a sports game, but not so great in a restaurant, at a drinks party, or anywhere that people are trying to relax.

Similarly, whispering is permissible once or twice at the theater, or even during the trailers at the movies, but should never happen at a gathering, or you run the risk that other guests will think you're talking about them and be offended.

So you see, talking the talk is really quite simple when you know how and have a few elegant pointers to help you on your way. So go forth and charm with your witty conversation and dulcet tones.

CHAPTER
2

WALK THE WALK

In this chapter, you'll learn:

❖ The key to positive body language ❖ The secrets of perfect posture
❖ How to stand and move like a lady ❖ How to use your body
language to influence others ❖ How to walk in high heels
❖ The ladylike way to sit

WHAT YOUR WALK
SAYS ABOUT YOU

It's not only supermodels who know that perfecting their walk and posture can make or break their reputation. While a catwalk strut might not be the stride we're striving for, it's a good example of how the way you hold yourself can illustrate the kind of image you wish to present. It's so much more than just putting one foot in front of the other. A confident pace, a brazen strut, a stiff march, a casual stroll, a heavy plod, an awkward shuffle—they all paint a picture of the kind of person you are before you've even uttered a word.

And it doesn't stop there. There's no point developing a superior stride if the moment you come to a standstill you drop into a slouch. Elegant poise gives an instant ladylike impression and demonstrates balance, composure, and self-possession. Just look at the way ballerinas carry themselves. Have you ever seen a dancer who appears anything other than the epitome of sophistication? Their apparent ease and naturally graceful posture give them a dignified appearance. But with a little effort, it is easy to emulate this chic stance and to have everyone in the room commenting on your presence and poise.

Great posture and poise have so many benefits—from helping your clothes to hang better and making you appear both taller and slimmer to illustrating your self-assurance, elegance, and grace. And the right walk and ability to sit correctly can not only help you land the job you want, but will also make you feel comfortable and confident at the most elegant of soirées. So step to it!

BODY TALK

Before you've opened your mouth, your body has started doing the talking for you. It's surprising how much we can communicate without even speaking, but just think about the message you send out with a frown, slouchy shoulders, or folded arms compared to a smile, a confident stance, or even a kiss. The way you hold and carry yourself reveals how you feel about yourself and how you feel about those around you.

In the last chapter we discussed how important it is for a lady to make those around her feel at ease and body language is a vital ingredient in this. Turning your back on someone, crossing your legs away from them, resting your head in your hand, and slumping in your seat while others talk to you can all give a person the impression that you don't want to be there. On the flipside, leaning in slightly when you talk to someone, making eye contact, smiling, and nodding are all physical ways to show you are interested and involved in a conversation.

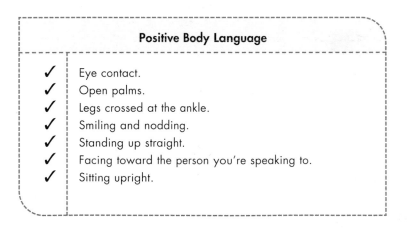

Positive Body Language

✓ Eye contact.
✓ Open palms.
✓ Legs crossed at the ankle.
✓ Smiling and nodding.
✓ Standing up straight.
✓ Facing toward the person you're speaking to.
✓ Sitting upright.

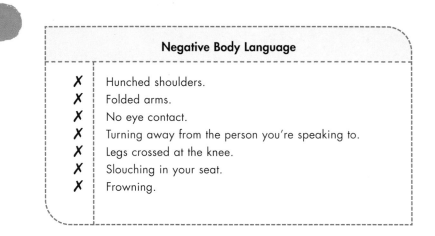

Negative Body Language

✗   Hunched shoulders.
✗   Folded arms.
✗   No eye contact.
✗   Turning away from the person you're speaking to.
✗   Legs crossed at the knee.
✗   Slouching in your seat.
✗   Frowning.

How to make a confident entrance

Have you ever been at a party and watched as a sophisticated woman enters the room: heads turn, she graces the gathering with a broad smile, making eye contact with a select few, before continuing in to join the throng. She immediately becomes the life of the party. You know it when you see it and all eyes are on the woman who can carry off a strong entrance that demonstrates self-confidence and style. The concept of "making an entrance" might be an old-fashioned one, since many social gatherings are now decidedly more casual, but if you can add this skill to your ladylike repertoire you'll grow at least an inch in self-confidence.

Making a classy entrance is simple if you remember a few key principles. Try these on for size.

Five Tips for Making an Award-winning Entrance

Natalie Glebova, Miss Universe 2005

1. Accomplish all petty tasks before crossing the threshold. Remove your coat, arrange stray hairs, blow your nose.

2. Avoid fumbling in your pockets, looking down, looking away, or looking angry.

3. Stand up straight and tall. Inhale deeply. Think: grace, confidence, elegance. Step through the doorway purposefully.

4. Enter then pause for a second, to make sweeping, wordless, and ever-so-brief eye contact with the occupants of the room.

5. Do not dally in the doorway. Move on and in. Extend a hand to shake, if appropriate, or pronounce a simple greeting to your new admirers.

PERFECT POISE AND POSTURE

It's all very well desiring the graceful poise of Darcey Bussell or Anna Pavlova, but as most of us don't have years of barre work behind us, we need to look at a few slightly simpler steps to develop the poise of a prima ballerina. As surprising as it may seem, teachers of the Alexander Technique—which releases unwanted tension in the muscles and helps you to develop better poise—suggest that perfect posture doesn't need to be learned, in fact young children often stand more correctly than adults. Because they are full of energy and have no unwanted tension, their muscles are not contracted, and then do not slump. They have not yet learned the lazy habits of adulthood which can cause curved spines, protruding bellies, or slumped shoulders. So the next time you are feel slouchy and lethargic, keep your eyes peeled for a tot and attempt to re-create their stance—weight balanced evenly, head looking upwardly and alert, body poised and perfect.

STAND TALL

The most essential thing to remember is to stand tall. Imagine a clothes hanger inside your jacket, which is keeping your shoulders pulled back and your chest slightly lifted. Now imagine the hanger has been hooked up behind you, so you lengthen your neck, keeping your upper body erect, and your rib cage lifted (this also helps you to breathe more easily). Keep your stomach pulled in and you bottom tucked under. Picture a plumb line hanging from your head all the way down your spine to the floor, and try to keep your shoulders and hips even so that it falls straight. All this may feel a bit awkward at first, but after a while you won't notice you're doing it. Whenever you remember, check your posture: take a deep breath to lift your rib cage and suck in your stomach, then stop your shoulders sagging forward by rolling them backward and down.

Fight the urge to lean on a piece of furniture or slump when you are on your feet. Keep your weight balanced equally between both of your feet and, as ballet dancers generally do, position your feet in the "third position"—with one foot in front of the other, front heel placed next to the middle of the back foot, and with the front foot turned slightly outward. Keep your arms comfortably by your sides and avoid crossing them or putting your hands on your hips.

Pilates and yoga teach correct body alignment and discourage lazy, sloppy posture. You might find a weekly class helpful not only for overall physical condition but in order to learn good posture habits. With improved posture and poise, you will present yourself as self-assured and on top of things rather than weighed down and tired.

SITTING

An overstuffed armchair is not an excuse to become a slob. Learn to sit well and you'll feel the benefits not just in your back and tummy muscles but your sense of self-confidence too.

Even Audrey Hepburn had to be taught how to sit up straight. According to her biographer, her grandmother tied her neck to the back of her chair at the table so she wouldn't slump. Sounds extreme? Then try a gentler method: practice good sitting posture by always keeping your back straight and crossing your legs at the ankle. At work, ensure you have an upright chair with a straight back, and avoid slouching over paperwork or the computer by keeping your feet firmly on the ground and your shoulders back and neck straight.

GETTING AROUND, OR, WHAT THEY USED TO CALL "DEPORTMENT"

 Deportment is such an old-fashioned word that conjures images of girls trying to walk while balancing dictionaries on their heads. It might be an old-fashioned idea, but a modern woman commands respect if she not only has good posture but carries herself erect and with confidence.

WALK WITH CONFIDENCE

A self-assured stride is a combination of good posture (which we've already mastered) and a purposeful walk. Your walk should be natural and not too stiff. There's no need to perfect it by balancing books on your head, but make sure it's not too casual either. Somewhere in between a geisha shuffle and a supermodel strut, you will find your perfect pace.

Always look ahead of you and not down at the ground. Don't make your steps too wide, and avoid pounding the pavement. Carry yourself lightly. The ability to glide across a room is synonymous with being a refined lady. Achieve this by keeping your knees soft when you walk and rolling your feet as they touch the ground, from the heel up to the toe, instead of slapping them down or shuffling around noisily. Avoid bouncing as you move and keep your body level to give the impression of walking smoothly. This is another maneuver that can be tricky to master, so practice when you walk past a reflective shop window—you want to keep yourself at a constant height as you go past. Let your arms hang freely beside you without letting them swing wildly around.

TO HAVE AND TO HOLD?

But what if you are walking with someone else? What level of physical contact is appropriate? Taking a stroll with your arm slung over someone's shoulder or your hand rammed into the back pocket of their jeans is very unladylike—but that's not to say that all contact is banned. Holding hands is definitely acceptable, whether your fingers are intertwined or hands clasped. So, for that matter, is linking arms. If a man offers you his arm, slip your hand inside the loop he creates with his arm and place your hand lightly on his forearm.

A gentleman should always walk closest to the road, between you and the traffic, but if he forgets this chivalrous detail, simply edge yourself to the inside anyway.

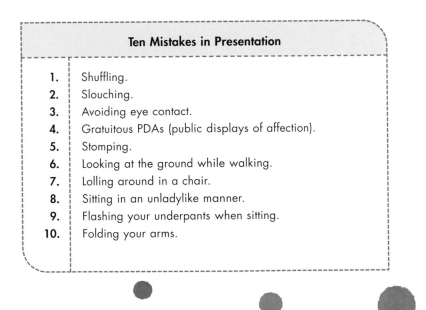

Ten Mistakes in Presentation

1. Shuffling.
2. Slouching.
3. Avoiding eye contact.
4. Gratuitous PDAs (public displays of affection).
5. Stomping.
6. Looking at the ground while walking.
7. Lolling around in a chair.
8. Sitting in an unladylike manner.
9. Flashing your underpants when sitting.
10. Folding your arms.

The Secret of a Successful Entrance to a Job Interview

This is a moment when confidence—but not cockiness—is essential. You want your body language to show potential employers that you are both self-assured and keen, but you need to be respectful at the same time. Follow these steps for a positive outcome—and hopefully a job offer!

Step One:	Take a moment to compose yourself before you enter the room.
Step Two:	Walk in at a reasonable pace, with a smile, and make eye contact with everyone as soon as you enter.
Step Three:	Remain standing and shake hands with each interviewer, keeping eye contact all the time.
Step Four:	When you have been offered a seat, perch yourself on your seat so that you are leaning forward slightly toward your prospective employers.
Step Five:	Keep your legs uncrossed and do not fold your arms over your chest, as both will make you appear reserved and unapproachable.
Step Six :	Angle your body toward whomever is asking you questions and make eye contact with everyone in the room while giving your answers.
Step Seven:	When you leave, do not stand up from your chair until your interviewers have done so, and shake hands with each person before leaving the room.

How to wear a suit

Suits are undeniably stylish and wearing one will give you instant panache. Add to this already elegant appearance by paying extra attention to your posture. Maintain the lines of a suit by keeping your shoulders back and by standing tall. When sitting, lift your trousers slightly to avoid the fabric pulling and if possible remove your jacket and hang it over the back of the chair to stop it from creasing.

The art of walking in high heels

They are essential in every lady's arsenal. They give a girl defined leg muscles and more importantly that extra boost to her confidence. But high heels also come with their own set of problems—standing, sitting, walking, and running! Here's a tip: the best place to practice walking in heels is your local supermarket—there are miles of aisles for getting used to the feel of heels and you can use your shopping cart for balance until you gain confidence.

With all the practice in the world, there will always be places where high heels become a potential death trap, so try to steer clear of cobbled streets, grating, and super-shiny marble floors, or opt for flats when you know these are unavoidable.

You can buy small gel pads to make your shoes more comfortable if you are wearing them for a long period of time, and it is sensible to slip a pair of ballet pumps into your handbag for emergencies—there is nothing less stylish than a girl hobbling with her feet covered in Band-Aids.

How to master stairs

Stairs can be tricky, especially when wearing heels and even more so if you are in a slim-fitting skirt. Conquer your fears of falling and master steps gracefully with these directives.

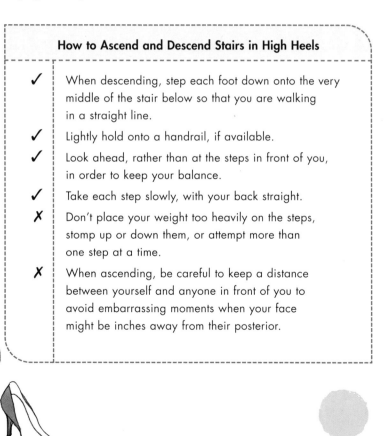

How to Ascend and Descend Stairs in High Heels

✓   When descending, step each foot down onto the very middle of the stair below so that you are walking in a straight line.

✓   Lightly hold onto a handrail, if available.

✓   Look ahead, rather than at the steps in front of you, in order to keep your balance.

✓   Take each step slowly, with your back straight.

✗   Don't place your weight too heavily on the steps, stomp up or down them, or attempt more than one step at a time.

✗   When ascending, be careful to keep a distance between yourself and anyone in front of you to avoid embarrassing moments when your face might be inches away from their posterior.

THE CAR MANEUVER

While celebrities may be happy to reveal all when emerging from a motor vehicle, ladies know that getting out of a car without flashing your underwear is a crucial skill to learn.

How to Get Out of a Car With Style

Step One:	Open the car door.
Step Two:	Edge your bottom all the way along the back seat, until you are balancing on just the corner.
Step Three:	Swing both legs out of the car together and place them firmly on the curb.
Step Four:	Use both hands to push down on the seat behind you and stand up.
Step Five:	If you happen to have a gentleman handy to help you out of the car, follow the same steps, but use just one hand to push yourself up and the other to take his hand in order to propel yourself forward.

THE LADYLIKE WAY TO SIT

Once you are out the car, the next task is sitting elegantly. Lowering yourself gently into a chair is more refined than plonking yourself down. Reach back to place one hand on the armrest and lower yourself down by bending your legs, while keeping your back as straight as possible. Avoid perching on the arm of a chair (some people are fussy about their furnishings) and, unless you're in your own home, do not curl your legs underneath you or put your feet up on the chair.

WHICH CHAIR TO GO FOR

Some chairs encourage unladylike posture—how can you concentrate on keeping your knees together and your back straight while sprawled on a

comfortable armchair? Similarly rocking chairs and beanbags are the enemy of any lady, and hammocks are impossible to get out of gracefully so should be avoided in company— and especially in a skirt! If you have a choice, opt for a chair that is slightly higher like a bar stool, and as stools are usually backless, they promote straight backs. Climbing down is also an easy and elegant maneuver.

Don't feel tempted to select a moving chair; twirling in a swivel chair, bouncing in a rocker, or kicking out a recliner are not much different from fidgeting, so should be avoided at all times. If you are sharing a seat, be wary of sticking to your side and not encroaching on someone else's space, and when you enter a room, be sure to hold back and let your companion choose their seat first. If this isn't an option, head to the least comfortable seat and give your pal the plum choice.

How to Sit in a Skirt

✓ Try to master the double-leg cross: Cross your legs at the knee then tuck the front foot behind the back ankle.

✓ Cross your legs at the ankle.

✓ Place your feet together and your legs parallel then drop them slightly to one side so one leg is balanced on top of the other.

How to Sit in Trousers

✓ Cross your legs at the ankle.

✓ Place your feet together on the floor and keep your knees together.

✗ Never balance one foot on the other knee so your legs are widely crossed or sit with your legs splayed, even in trousers.

CHAPTER 3

GROOMING AND STYLE

In this chapter, you'll learn:

❦ How to build an outfit ❦ Which colors suit you best
❦ Which items are a must in your wardrobe ❦ How to accessorize
❦ How to dress for the occasion ❦ Good grooming
❦ Monthly maintenance

THE LOOK OF A LADY

Fabulous style is the one thing every woman would love to possess. Few are naturally born with it—Jackie Onassis, Audrey Hepburn, Kate Moss. The rest of us might have to try a little harder, but the simple fact is, if you wear the right outfit you'll fit in anywhere.

While innate style is a gift, alongside a great singing voice or legs that go on for miles, unlike the latter two qualities, you can develop your own signature look with a little self-confidence and experience. Learning which colors, styles and shapes suit you best and becoming a savvy shopper will help you to look fantastic in whatever you wear. It takes confidence to create your own distinctive sense of style, but the rewards are that you'll be able to assess easily if something is "you" or not, and others will recognize your style and respect you for it.

In this chapter we explore the essence of dressing well, how to make the most of your figure, how to build a fail-safe wardrobe around those key items, and how to put together the appropriate outfit for the occasion. We also discuss how to carve out your own signature look, how to avoid making a fashion faux pas, what to pack for a vacation, and how to fix any fashion foibles.

And let's not forget grooming: bed head and smudged lipstick have no place in the beauty regime of a lady. From finding your trademark scent to distinguishing your day from evening makeup effects, we focus on how good grooming can be a simple affair, which enables you to look your best each time you open your front door. Ready for a lesson in looking like a lady?

How to build an outfit

As with most things, how you feel on the inside dictates how you look on the outside, so the most important thing about the clothes you wear is that they make you feel good. This could be because you know they make the most of your figure, you love the feeling of the fabric, or you are attracted to the detail or color. A pair of black pants can be cut beautifully, a sweater made of the softest cashmere, a T-shirt in a glorious hue that perfectly matches your eyes, and a pair of flat ballet pumps scattered with rhinestone gems. Never buy anything solely on the basis that is it functional and it fits—you should no less than adore everything in your closet. Otherwise, let's face it, you won't get the use out of it and it will just clutter up your storage space.

When you are building a wardrobe from scratch, stick to one or two shades that suit you best, and choose key pieces, such as straight-leg pants, A-line skirts, cardigans and sweaters, T-shirts, and tank tops.

Details That Make Any Item a Must-buy

✓   A super-flattering cut, which enhances your figure.
✓   A classic item in a luxury fabric such as cashmere or silk.
✓   A unique shade of your favorite color.
✓   Elegant embellishments such as embroidery,
     quirky buttons, gems, or a contrasting trim.

COLOR CODE

The right shade will make your skin glow, your hair look more glossy, and your eyes sparkle; on the flipside, wearing a color that is wrong for you can turn your outfit from fab to drab. When choosing which shade to buy, bear two things in mind: which color flatters your complexion and which reflects your personality. Below is a quick guide to identifying the hues that suit you, depending on your skin and hair color.

Hair color and Complexion	Colors That Suit
Blonde; fair complexion	Baby blue, cornflower blue, bright pink, grass green, cream, navy
Brunette; olive skin	Smoky gray, fire-engine red, black, violet, coral pink
Black hair; dark skin	Sunshine yellow, orange, white, silver, gold, magenta
Red hair; fair complexion	Olive green, deep purple and burgundy, chocolate brown, beige, petrol blue

DRESSING TO SUIT YOUR SHAPE

Genevieve Antoine Dariaux wrote in her 1964 style tome *Elegance: A Complete Guide for Every Woman Who Wants to be Well and Properly Dressed on all Occasions*: "the feminine figure is either an I or an O, or any one of the infinite number of intermediate stages. There are very few fashion problems for the Is, but plenty of them for the Os." Over four decades later the same rules still apply: While lithe, leggy girls manage to look fabulous with little effort, curvier women seem to struggle more in the style stakes. But actresses Kate Winslet and Scarlett Johansson prove that learning to dress to flatter your figure means you can look gorgeous, whatever vowel you emulate.

The basic rule to keep in mind is to draw attention away from the areas of your body you are not happy with, and toward the areas that you are.

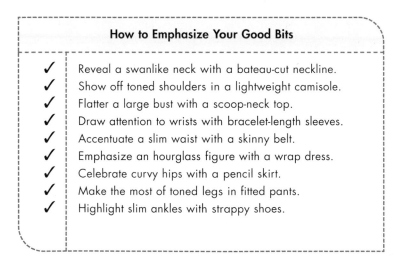

How to Emphasize Your Good Bits

✓ Reveal a swanlike neck with a bateau-cut neckline.
✓ Show off toned shoulders in a lightweight camisole.
✓ Flatter a large bust with a scoop-neck top.
✓ Draw attention to wrists with bracelet-length sleeves.
✓ Accentuate a slim waist with a skinny belt.
✓ Emphasize an hourglass figure with a wrap dress.
✓ Celebrate curvy hips with a pencil skirt.
✓ Make the most of toned legs in fitted pants.
✓ Highlight slim ankles with strappy shoes.

Dress for respect

Read any fashion magazine and they'll tell you that less is more—that you may wear a miniskirt, or a low-cut top, but never the two together. A lady knows that neither a skirt that barely covers underwear, nor a top that reveals plunging depths of cleavage, is appropriate.

It's fine to give a hint of décolletage, but draw attention to your collarbones rather than your bust—any more than an inch of cleavage is too much. As for skirts and shorts, never go higher than two inches above the knee. If you're in between sizes, always purchase the larger of the two—no one will look at the label, and clothes that give you room to move are more slimming than those you have to squeeze into. Following are five more timeless rules for avoiding fashion disasters.

Be stylish not slutty

Certain items of clothing can look stylish or slutty depending upon how they're worn. A chiffon shirt is elegant with a camisole in the same shade underneath, but uncouth when worn with just a bra. A glimpse of fishnet pantyhose from the hem of a cigarette pant is stylish, but paired with a knee-length skirt they're just trashy.

Be style savvy without becoming a fashion victim

If you love designer labels, avoid the dominant prints or the pieces that have appeared in every fashion magazine, as these will date quickly.

If in doubt, keep it classic

Shift dresses, black pants, and ballet flats are timeless; the must-have fashion item of the season not.

Do your research

Find out what your host is wearing before going to a party, to avoid stealing their thunder in an identical ensemble.

Less is more

Coco Chanel implored women to take off one accessory before leaving the house. This advice is still golden. But remember also that your body is an accessory in itself—a large bust doesn't need adornment with a big necklace.

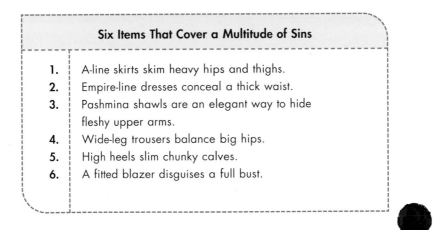

Six Items That Cover a Multitude of Sins

1. A-line skirts skim heavy hips and thighs.
2. Empire-line dresses conceal a thick waist.
3. Pashmina shawls are an elegant way to hide fleshy upper arms.
4. Wide-leg trousers balance big hips.
5. High heels slim chunky calves.
6. A fitted blazer disguises a full bust.

WARDROBE ESSENTIALS

So you know the colors and styles that suit you. You know the patterns and prints that attract you. But do you have the wardrobe basics that stand the test of time and form the backbone of your collection?

A **BLACK** DRESS

Also known as the LBD (little black dress), this item of clothing has become synonymous with style and elegance (who can forget Holly Golightly's shift dress in *Breakfast at Tiffany's?*). The key to choosing a LBD that will never date is to find a classic cut that suits your figure in an enduring fabric. Beanpoles look best in sleeveless shifts with bateau necklines; curvy girls should look for dresses with elbow-length sleeves and scooped necklines. In terms of fabric, you'll never go wrong with a dress made from jersey silk, charmeuse, peau de soie (double-faced satin), or quality cashmere.

CRISP WHITE T-SHIRT

You can never have too many white tees and they go perfectly with everything—from jeans to dress pants, and flip-flops to stilettos. As no T-shirt stays crisp and white forever, you should expect to replace yours every few months. For this reason, don't spend a fortune on them, but at the same time look out for tees with a twist, such as with buttons, interesting stitching, or cap sleeves.

SMART JEANS

The one piece of clothing that no girl can live without is her denims—but avoid anything faded, bleached, stone-washed, or too baggy. Smart jeans should be a dark indigo blue, have a straight-leg cut, without a low-cut waistband. Look for a pair with a little bit of stretch to hug your figure and, if you can afford it, buy another pair that stop at your ankle, to wear with ballet pumps and flat sandals, and another a few inches longer, to be worn with heels.

HIGH HEELS

These creations are responsible for making any girl look taller, her legs look slimmer, and her feet look more elegant. You can build an entire outfit around a divine pair of heels—try black cigarette pants and a black polo-neck sweater with a pair of turquoise heels, or a demure gray chiffon gown with some bejeweled magenta stilettos. A three-inch heel is the perfect height—tall enough to enhance your posture, but not so tottering that you are risking a Naomi Campbell-esque fall. Every closet should contain at least three pairs: black court shoes, tan heels, and silver strappy sandals.

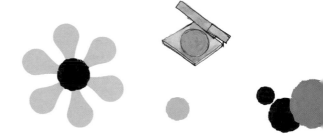

What lies beneath

The most beautiful dress can be ruined by one thing: lumpy, bumpy underwear. Bras that bulge and visible panty lines are two things every lady should learn how to combat.

Start by separating your lingerie into two categories: the pieces that should be seen in public and the pieces that shouldn't. Contrary to the past, it is no longer considered bad etiquette to show off some of your lingerie. A vintage silk camisole looks beautiful worn with a cashmere cardigan and pencil skirt, and bra straps that are adored with lace and chiffon are made to be seen. Choose soft shades, though—scarlet or hot pink scream "harlot," so stick to hues of blush, oyster and pale gray instead.

As for never-to-be-seen-in-public lingerie, opt for a peach or flesh-colored shade, which will be invisible under the sheerest top, and choose seamless pieces that are unadorned. While G-string briefs are not as glamourous as frilly underpants, they are a much more sensible choice under slim-fit pants. Similarly, a T-shirt bra, with no lace or trimmings, might be dull to look at, but don't underestimate its powers; it will create a smooth line when worn under a blouse or tee.

How to choose the right bra

Many women don't wear the correct size bra. Just look around and you'll notice breasts escaping over the top of too-small cups, too-tight straps squeezing back flesh, or floppy breasts barely held in by a saggy, too-large bra. It really is worth the bother to get yourself properly measured in a lingerie store. Brands and styles can fit differently, so try a few on before making a decision.

Bras should never dig into your shoulders (loosen the straps), squeeze your ribs, or create unsightly bulges in your back (go up a size around the back). Larger busts need more support, so stick to underwire bras with at least two hook closures and thicker shoulder straps.

Big cup sizes don't necessarily mean ugly bras. Look for distinguished brands that make glamourous bras in larger sizes. Invest in a few of these and they will make a big difference to your shape and the way your clothing hangs. But if you have a small bust and don't require so much support, experiment with wireless bras, bandeau tops, and details such as bows, ruffles and embroidery.

The Undergarments Every Woman Should Own

- ✓ Black strapless bra.
- ✓ Flesh-colored T-shirt bra.
- ✓ Balcony-cut bra.
- ✓ Multiway bra.
- ✓ Sports bra.
- ✓ Pretty camisole with matching underpants.
- ✓ Boyshorts.
- ✓ Flesh-colored G-string.
- ✓ Cotton briefs.
- ✓ Black slip.
- ✓ Blush slip.

IF THE SHOE FITS

While every girl needs her high heels, these aren't the only must-haves that demand a place in a lady's arsenal. Ballet flats, loved by Audrey

Hepburn and Kate Moss, are elegant, easy to wear and work with everything from skirts to jeans to capri pants. For summer, look for flat sandals as a chic alternative to rubber flip-flops. Loafers are also timeless—buy a pair in the softest leather you can find. Knee-high boots are essential in the winter and, while a high-heeled pair can be worn in the evening too, a flat equestrian boot is a stylish alternative for daywear. Leave training shoes for the gym and instead opt for canvas sneakers if you want a classic casual look.

HOW TO ACCESSORIZE

Beautiful accessories can transform an outfit and form the distinguishing feature of a lady's personal style. One of the simplest ways to pull off an outfit is to wear well-cut classic pieces but to give your look a twist with quirky accents. While fuchsia pants and a green patterned blouse might be garish, a silk scarf in the same print but paired with classic, neutral clothes can look stunning. Don't worry about finding accessories to match your outfits—if you dress in a neutral palette, your shoes, bags, scarves and jewellery will bring the look to life. So have fun building a collection of interesting pieces and don't forget to visit vintage stores for gorgeous scarves, brooch pins and costume jewelry that no one else will have.

If you dare, this is also a great opportunity to make some bolder style statements. White gloves or hats with little net veils may not be the height of fashion anymore, but they are quintessentially ladylike, and in the right environment become make-an-outfit pieces. Try wearing white gloves to a summer garden party or wedding and donning a small headpiece with a black net veil along with a simple black dress to a cocktail party.

One word of warning, however: remember that the real secret to making accessories work for you is to wear them sparingly. Choose either dangly earrings or a big necklace, but not both. A long pendant should not have to complete with a brooch pin. A cocktail ring shouldn't jostle for room alongside an armful of bangles. A colorful bag worn with equally bright shoes is just too much. See your clothes as a canvas and your accessories as artwork, and let each piece get the exhibition it deserves.

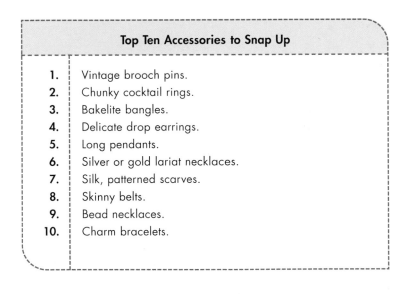

Top Ten Accessories to Snap Up

1. Vintage brooch pins.
2. Chunky cocktail rings.
3. Bakelite bangles.
4. Delicate drop earrings.
5. Long pendants.
6. Silver or gold lariat necklaces.
7. Silk, patterned scarves.
8. Skinny belts.
9. Bead necklaces.
10. Charm bracelets.

Handbag style

There are so many bags to choose from and so many different occasions that call for one. Even if your budget is limited, you'll still need two bags: a medium-sized shoulder bag in a sturdy fabric such as  leather or canvas and in a neutral color such as black, gray, brown, or navy for day; and a small evening bag in a more special fabric such as satin or velvet for the evening. Of course, if you have more to spend, the options are endless and the choosing is half the fun! Just remember the rules: one larger bag is always better than two or three smaller ones; don't buy a bag too large because you'll be tempted to fill it; and spend as much as you can afford on a quality, classic look. Below are some suggestions for matching the appropriate bag to the situation:

Situation	Type of Bag
Work	Medium-to-large leather bag with shoulder strap.
Weekend	Small-to-medium canvas tote or messenger bag.
Gym	Medium-sized hold-all or rucksack in canvas or twill.
Party	Small clutch in a bright color with embellishments.
Black tie	Small clutch or drawstring bag in dark shade with chic details.

WHAT'S IN YOUR HANDBAG?

If you drop your handbag, does an assortment of half-eaten cookies, used tissues and long-forgotten notes and receipts cascade out? Are you always scratching around in your bag for a pen and scribbling appointments on your hand? Act like a lady and you'll pare back the contents of your bag to the essentials. Here are the basic must-have contents of any lady's handbag:

Inside a Lady's Handbag
✓ Wallet.
✓ Keys.
✓ Cell phone.
✓ Diary.
✓ Lipstick.
✓ Small hairbrush.
✓ Perfume.
✓ Tissues.
✓ Good pen.
✓ Small notebook.
✓ Chewing gum or breath freshener.
✓ Band-Aids.
✓ Painkillers.
✓ Tampons.
✓ Spare pair of pantyhose.
✓ Mini umbrella (if you have room).

DRESSING FOR THE OCCASION

You might have a closet full of designer garments and the jewels of royalty, but if you don't know how to dress for the occasion, you'll never look like a lady. When you turn up at an event wearing inappropriate dress, your confidence plummets. So consider the following pointers for creating killer combinations for the right situation.

THE JOB INTERVIEW

It's always elegant to opt for a skirt when attending a job interview. Even if you are being interviewed for a position at a creative company, avoid jeans and dress up more than you would normally. It's safer to go for a more formal option than a casual one. This doesn't mean that you can't still express your personality. A pencil skirt with a fine-gauge sweater and a quirky silk scarf or unique brooch pin is just perfect. Heels are fine, but not too high, and pantyhose are more acceptable than bare legs. Invest in a timeless but stylish coat and bag for these occasions too.

THE FIRST DATE

Choose an outfit that's casual, a little bit sexy, and effortless—you want to look like you've made an effort, but haven't been planning your ensemble for hours. Wear those smart jeans along with a silk camisole or sheer blouse under a cashmere cardigan. A fine necklace that draws attention to your throat and a pair of heels will make you look even more glamorous.

THE AIRPLANE

Dressing for travel is never easy—although you want to be comfortable, it's still important to look smart (especially if you are hoping for an upgrade!). Wear a smart pair of jeans—if they are not too comfortable, you can always roll up a pair of jersey bottoms in your carry-on bag to slip into once onboard. (Liz Hurley, who always looks impeccable in an airport, changes into pajamas on the plane!) A long-sleeved T-shirt, light sweater and loafers complete the outfit, along with a pair of thick socks and a pashmina that can double as a blanket to protect against fierce air-conditioning. If you choose items in basic colors that can easily be mixed and matched, you have no need to end up with an over-packed, unwieldy suitcase.

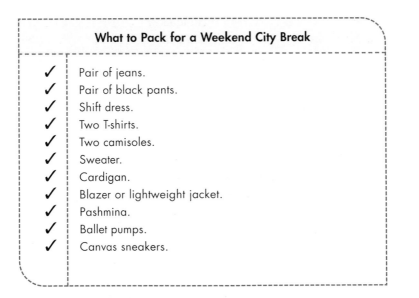

What to Pack for a Weekend City Break

- ✓ Pair of jeans.
- ✓ Pair of black pants.
- ✓ Shift dress.
- ✓ Two T-shirts.
- ✓ Two camisoles.
- ✓ Sweater.
- ✓ Cardigan.
- ✓ Blazer or lightweight jacket.
- ✓ Pashmina.
- ✓ Ballet pumps.
- ✓ Canvas sneakers.

What to Wear if the Invitation Says . . .

White tie/evening dress	White tuxedos for men and floor-length evening gowns (with gloves if you desire) for women.
Black tie	Black dinner jackets for men and cocktail dresses for women. Your dress doesn't need to be long, but never go above the knee.
Smart day/formal day dress	Men should wear jackets or blazers and ties; women should wear dresses or very formal pants with a dressy blouse.
Smart casual	Don't wear jeans. Men should stick to pants and a button-down shirt; a blazer is optional. For women, a chic summer dress and flat sandals or smart pants and an embellished sweater would both be suitable.
Come as you are	This doesn't mean in your sweatpants and slippers! Jeans are fine for both men and women; team yours with a pretty blouse and jeweled flats.

GOOD GROOMING

There's no point dressing the part if you have badly applied makeup and ratty hair. But on the other hand, when it comes to being ladylike, the less-is-more approach is always best. Glossy, healthy hair and flawless skin, free from heavy makeup, should be your goal.

THE BASIC TOOLS

Start with good-quality makeup applicators and hairbrush. Even if you buy cheap makeup, it's worth spending a little extra on the applicators. Good-quality applicators will last years; bad-quality brushes will lose their bristles the first day you use them and will drive you mad.

EVERYDAY GROOMING

While you'll want to make an effort for big occasions, it's easier to really impress if you maintain your skin and hair in between.

As for your skin, remove your makeup every night with a cream or foaming cleanser, clarify skin with a toner, and finish with a good moisturizer. There really is no getting around this routine. The two-in-one products just don't cut it. Every morning apply a light moisturizer with SPF before the rest of your makeup.

While each hair type is different, and a salon can recommend the best way to care for yours, fine hair should be washed daily with a mild shampoo, normal hair should be washed every other day, and thick or frizzy hair, which can often be tamed by your scalp's natural oils, can be left for up to a week between washes.

YOUR LOOK: DAY

Start with a light foundation to even out your skin tone. To create a lighter formula, mix it with a little moisturizer before applying, or apply it only to your T-zone (across your forehead and down your nose and chin—this is where your skin is oiliest). Hide dark circles or blemishes with a light concealer. It's worth spending money on a good-quality one that blends perfectly with your skin tone. Curl your eyelashes (even if you don't plan to wear mascara) to draw attention to your eyes. Finish with a lick of black or brown mascara, depending on your coloring. Have your eyelashes tinted for color that lasts six weeks. Apply a natural-looking blush to the apples of your cheeks (peachy or light pink shades are better than strong pinks or bronzes) and finish with a slick of lightly tinted lip gloss.

YOUR LOOK: NIGHT

The same foundation rules apply as above. A heavy mask of base is never appealing, but to help your makeup last all night you could finish with a dusting of translucent powder. Conceal your dark rings or blemishes as above. Try a smoky eye by smudging dark gray or navy eye shadow along your lash line. A single line of black liquid eyeliner along your top lashes is a timeless beauty trick and a light dusting of a bone-colored eye shadow containing a little shimmer is a subtle but elegant look. Or if you want to wear a bold-colored eye shadow, opt for simply lining the lash line with a brown liner and smudging it with a fingertip. Always finish the look with a few coats of mascara. A dusting of blush is again in order, or you could smudge a little cream blush onto your cheekbones. Play up your lips more at night, but remember the rule that you Emphasize either your eyes or your lips, never both.

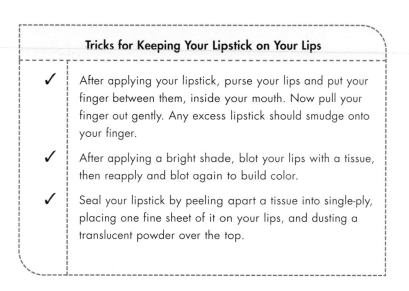

Tricks for Keeping Your Lipstick on Your Lips

✓ After applying your lipstick, purse your lips and put your finger between them, inside your mouth. Now pull your finger out gently. Any excess lipstick should smudge onto your finger.

✓ After applying a bright shade, blot your lips with a tissue, then reapply and blot again to build color.

✓ Seal your lipstick by peeling apart a tissue into single-ply, placing one fine sheet of it on your lips, and dusting a translucent powder over the top.

YOUR MONTHLY OVERHAUL

Good grooming is all about maintenance. Keep to your everyday routine and you'll avoid bad-skin and -hair days, but if you're able to make it to a monthly overhaul at your favourite beauty salon, you'll always look your best. It may sound extreme, but if you keep it up you will reap the benefits by not only looking but feeling great. If you're worried about the money aspect, just think how much you would spend on an average night out on the town (which may be a depressing thought in itself!), and go out once less a month. To ensure you always get an appointment, schedule your dates at the beginning of the year and pencil yourself in for the same date and time every month. Experts advise you have these treatments at the following regularity:

Treatment	Regularity
Manicure	Every two to four weeks.
Pedicure	Every two to four weeks in summer.
Waxing	Every three weeks.
Facial	Monthly.
Eyelash tint	Every six weeks.
Hair trim	Every two months.
Highlights	Every three months.

HOW TO FIND YOUR SIGNATURE SCENT

Leaving a gentle waft of a heavenly scent in your wake is such a lovely way to be remembered, but in order to do so, you must find a scent that speaks to you. The best way to do this is to spend an afternoon trying different perfumes to see which one most appeals to you. Do you prefer a light, flowery scent or something more heady and spicy?

To find something unusual, avoid the big designer brands and head to stores that produce their own distinctive blends using essential oils. Wear your scent lighter by day and in the summer—use an eau de toilette rather than a perfume, or a scented shower gel or moisturizer. In the winter or at night, choose something heavier.

Grooming dilemmas

It's impossible to avoid grooming dilemmas completely, so here's a few precious tips on how to fix them with minimal fuss.

Your mascara runs

Carry a cotton ball and a travel-sized bottle of cleanser in your handbag if you're worried about this. Dip the cotton ball into the cream and rub under your eye to clean off the mascara without affecting the rest of your lashes. Then invest in a waterproof mascara.

Your heel breaks

One answer is to carry a pair of ballet pumps in your bag to slip on in emergencies. If this is not an option, place the weight on the ball of your foot while walking, until you get to the shoe shop!

Your pantyhose run

If you don't have a spare pair in your bag and the run is very small, dab the end with a little clear nail polish to stop it from getting worse. If it is a dramatic, visible run, remove your tights—bare legs are preferable.

You drop oil down the front of your top

Soak up any excess with a paper napkin. Try to conceal the mark with a scarf, by re-pinning a brooch pin, or covering with a cardigan. This is when a friend with a spare cardigan or jacket is most handy.

CHAPTER
4

HOSTING AND DINING

In this chapter, you'll learn:

✦ How to be the life of the party ✦ How to be the perfect guest
✦ Flawless table manners ✦ How to tackle tricky foods
✦ How to deal with dining dilemmas ✦ How to be the perfect
hostess ✦ Serving ideas for scrumptious spreads

HOW TO BE THE LIFE OF THE PARTY

What imagery does the idea of being a good hostess conjure? A 1950s housewife offering a plate of canapés to a select group of guests before calmly serving a three-course meal? A charming, well-dressed, well-mannered woman working a crowded room, topping up glasses, and ensuring everyone at the party is engaged in convivial conversation?

Kitsch though these images may be, they capture the essence of the hospitality and generosity of spirit that is at the heart of being a modern lady. A busy work schedule, a small apartment, and the relative ease of eating fast food need not prevent you from developing your skills as a hostess. You don't need a glamorous location and extravagant food to host a chic soirée. Learn how to be a fabulous hostess without the frenzy. Make an invitation to your place the hottest ticket in town, whether it's for tea and cake, or cocktails and canapés.

But what does it matter how you behave as a guest? When invited to a special occasion, you need to understand the unstated rules of behavior. You want to be the one guest without whom no party is complete. A little attention to such things as table manners and party-guest decorum might seem old-fashioned, but when you know how to eat your soup and oysters without ruining your clothing, when you can elegantly negotiate demanding dinner-party conversation, it will pay off many times over. Friends and acquaintances will be charmed by your company and you'll find the biggest problem you have is squeezing all the social engagements into your calendar.

PARTY POSSIBILITIES

So you have received an invitation from a friend to a social gathering but are not sure of the protocol. Read on for an idea of what to expect at various occasions.

BRUNCH

A combination of breakfast and lunch, this is often an array of both sweet and savory dishes. It could include homemade muesli or granola with yogurt and fresh fruit, warm bagels or croissants, smoked salmon or bacon and scrambled eggs. Always served with plenty of coffee, you might also find yourself offered a Bloody Mary cocktail or champagne on a special occasion.

BUFFET

Usually a lunchtime affair, a buffet is an informal get-together. Casual attire is fine. Check in with your host or hostess before the event to see if they would like you to bring a dish to add to the communal feast. If the answer is yes, try to bring something homemade. Desserts are always a good bet—a fruit salad or a huge bowl of berries with fresh mint are simple but always welcome, while an old-fashioned trifle or profiteroles are invariably crowd pleasers and go a long way. If you can't bear the idea of cooking, hit the deli and buy olives, feta, sun-dried tomatoes, and marinated artichokes to create an antipasti platter. Never be the first in line for a buffet and do not overfill your plate. Going up for seconds shows enthusiasm, thirds shows gluttony!

AFTERNOON TEA

An excuse to cut crusts off sandwiches! This is a British-style afternoon "high tea." You might find cucumber, egg, or poached salmon sandwiches cut into fingers. There may be scones with cream and jam and there will always be a selection of cakes served on tiered platters.

Remember that the treats are for all the guests to share and never serve yourself more than three pieces at a time—it's quite acceptable to come back for more but not to pile your bread-and-butter plate high. Endless cups of tea are the order of the day at a soirée such as this and sometimes even pink champagne.

Suddenly hip again, afternoon tea parties are the perfect way to celebrate an engagement or reunion of friends. To go with the fancy, frilly food, wear something suitably girly. Take a pretty gift for your host, from a posy of sweet peas to a deliciously scented candle.

COCKTAIL PARTY

This is your chance to dress to impress. Anything from a gorgeous sequined camisole worn with skinny cigarette pants to a shift dress with sparkly shoes is the norm. Showing up slightly late here could be beneficial. Arrive between 15 and 30 minutes after the stated arrival time to give the hostess a chance to finish those last-minute touches.

Don't bring flowers—your hostess will be far too busy refreshing drinks to worry about vases and water. A bottle of wine or even vodka (especially if it's in an elaborate, stylish bottle) makes a far better and more useful gift. Don't stay too late or drink too much; work the room and you'll be the life and soul of the party.

FORMAL DINNER PARTY

A dinner party traditionally consists of appetizers served with drinks as guests arrive, followed by at least three courses: a starter, main course, and dessert. Cheese and/or coffee and chocolates afterward are an elegant touch, but not essential.

Remember that it's advisable to arrive around 15 minutes after the indicated time, but never so late that the party is forced to wait a long time having drinks before they can start the meal.

If you're lucky enough to be invited to something so old-school, remember that the old rules apply. Social graces are essential; be demure and a little reserved. If in doubt, follow the lead of those around you. That means waiting for them to head to the dining table, seeing which set of cutlery they use, and rising for speeches and toasts when they do, if appropriate.

Dress demurely too—a long dress is the order of the day. At a formal dinner, there is no need to bring a bottle of wine, but a gift for the hostess is always a nice gesture.

One more word of advice: pace yourself with the food. There may be more courses than you think.

SUPPER

This is a casual and often impromptu get-together. Most likely served later than a dinner would be, it's a light meal consisting perhaps of such offerings as a cheese board, bread, pâté, and soup. Don't expect to fill up on a substantial meal but if the conversation flows effortlessly, you can expect a late night.

WEDDING

It is always an honor to be invited to a wedding—it's such an important occasion for the hosts and their close family, even if they choose a relatively informal way to celebrate it. And of course weddings demand more careful observation of a few basic rules of etiquette than do most other occasions.

Reply to your invitation as soon as possible to inform the hosts of your availability. It is very bad manners not to respond to a wedding invitation by the RSVP date.

Make a note of the dress code—a black-tie or evening wedding will require a more formal outfit than a day wedding. Trousers are not quite formal enough for a wedding—stick to a dress or an elegant skirt and top. Try to avoid wearing black, which is too somber, or white, which is the bride's domain (unless, of course, you are asked to wear either, which is quite de rigueur these days). A British wedding almost always calls for a hat, though nowadays a feather fascinator, flourish, or veiled headband are just as acceptable and stylish. If the ceremony is in a church, bring a shawl or wrap to cover bare shoulders.

When it comes to gifts, you can take yours along on the day, however many couples now inform their guests of a gift registry in advance, in which case gifts are bought and sent often before the nuptials. If friends inform you of a gift registry, act early so you will have the pick of the gifts (and so you don't end up with a dishcloth and lemon squeezer as your offerings). Protocol in the United States insists you have up to a year after the event to send your gift, but it is dangerous to assume this, so be prepared with your gift before the Big Day.

Finally, while a wedding isn't a wedding without that one person who guzzles too much champagne, goes wild on the dance floor, or ends up flirting outrageously with the best man, don't let it be you. Remember to eat beforehand if there will be hours between the ceremony and dinner, and to keep an eye on your bubbly consumption.

FUNERAL

These somber occasions can be both painful and difficult to navigate. They can be an emotional minefield, so the best idea is to keep a low profile and offer a shoulder to anyone who needs it. While dark colors should most certainly be worn, dark gray or navy are now just as appropriate as black.

Send a condolence card immediately after the bereavement and flowers to the church or crematorium. Think about making a phone call to show your support if appropriate.

At the wake, you probably won't feel in the mood to work the room, but this is an occasion on which you shouldn't. This isn't an occasion for building new friendships; instead see if you can make yourself useful by making gallons of tea and helping out wherever you can. Some wakes are seen as a celebration of the person's life and therefore tend to be lighter in tone—you should still offer to help out here, instead of tearing up the dancefloor with Uncle Jim.

BEING THE PERFECT GUEST . . .

If you want your name on every guest list, perfect the art of being an effortless partygoer. Start by investing in two elegant sets of stationery—one to RSVP to all your invitations and the second to send as thank-yous after the event. And always take a gift. Instead of the more usual wine and flowers, you could try gorgeous soap or hand cream in stylish packaging, a flowering plant in a pot, gourmet cheese and a jar of chutney, a DVD of a classic movie, the latest must-read book, multicolored macaroons, or a heavenly scented candle. The main rule is to be inventive!

AND WHAT TO DO IF YOU AREN'T . . .

Whether you arrive late, spill a glass of wine, or call someone by the wrong name, there are always ways to turn a dire first impression into a mere forgettable awkwardness that won't sully your reputation. Apologize immediately, but not dramatically; try not to bring any more attention to yourself. If you have spilled a drink or broken something, offer to pay for the cleaning or mending. Also send a handwritten note the following day, accompanied by a bunch of flowers. A few hours later, follow up with a phone call. The flowers will have had a softening effect and it's better to make verbal contact within a day or two rather than leaving the matter to brew until the next time you see each other.

Fifteen Ways to Be the Ideal Party Guest

1.   Reply to an invitation promptly.
2.   Dress for the occasion and make an effort.
3.   Arrive around 15 minutes after the "start" time.
4.   Bring the hostess a gift as well as something to drink.
5.   Greet the host and thank them for the invitation.
6.   Make an effort to socialize with people new to you.
7.   Work the room and chat to as many people as you can.
8.   Help create a party atmosphere with jokes and anecdotes you know everyone will enjoy.
9.   Offer your services to the host, whether it be passing around canapés or topping up glasses.
10. Listen to the hostess's requests, head to the dining room when she requests, or hit the dance floor so others will follow suit.
11. Don't flirt inappropriately.
12. Don't smoke in the house or drink red wine near pale-colored furnishings.
13. Judge when the party is winding down and make a move to leave—try not to be the first or the last to head home.
14. Offer to help with any cleaning-up before departing.
15. Always send an e-mail or a card the following day to say thank you for the wonderful time you had.

TABLE MANNERS

It might have been a while since your parents drummed correct table manners into you, so a quick refresher course is no bad thing. Remember, this is less about adhering to some archaic set of rules and more about showing respect to those around you and letting your conversation and sparkling company shine through, unimpeded by rude and distracting behavior. Here are the golden rules:

The Golden Rules of Table Decorum

✓ Start with good posture: Don't slouch over your food. Sit up straight in your chair and do not rest your elbows on the table.

✗ Don't fidget, play with your napkin, or peel candle wax off the tablecloth.

✓ Wait until everyone is seated before starting your food.

✗ Don't season your food until you've tried it.

✓ Eat by bringing your fork or spoon up to your mouth, rather than lowering your mouth down to your plate.

✓ Ask for food to be passed to you rather than reaching over people.

✓ Do rest your knife and fork in between bites so you don't rush your food.

✗ Try not to leave food on your plate, as this could offend your host.

How to Use a Napkin

Step One:	Lay a napkin over your lap; never tuck it into your shirt!
Step Two:	Bring it up to your lips to dab them lightly rather than rubbing them.
Step Three:	If you leave the table during a meal, leave your napkin on your seat until you return.
Step Four:	Once you have finished eating, put your napkin on the table, to the side of your dirty plate—never on top.

How to Handle Your Cutlery

✓ Navigate your cutlery by starting with the ones on the outside and working your way in. If in doubt, wait for others to pick theirs up first and follow their lead.

✓ If only a fork is provided (with risotto, for example), you may use it in your right hand with the prongs facing upward, like a spoon; otherwise, use it in your left hand, prongs facing downward, with a knife.

✓ After you've finished eating, lay your knife and fork side by side in the middle of your plate with the handles pointed toward you and with the prongs of the fork pointing upward.

✗ Never put your knife in your mouth!

How to Open a Bottle of Wine

Step One:	Vertically screw down the corkscrew into the center of the cork, all the way in.
Step Two:	Steadily and slowly lever or pull the cork up and out with the corkscrew, when you'll hear the pop. In informal company, you might clasp the bottle between your legs, if necessary, for better leverage.
Step Three:	If the cork breaks, start again. Rescue and discreetly discard any floating cork from the glass before handing out.

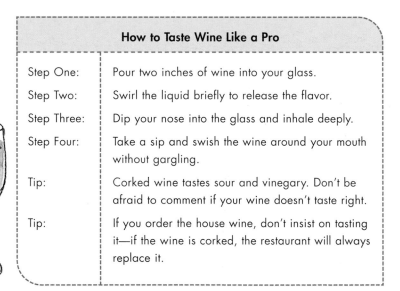

How to Taste Wine Like a Pro

Step One:	Pour two inches of wine into your glass.
Step Two:	Swirl the liquid briefly to release the flavor.
Step Three:	Dip your nose into the glass and inhale deeply.
Step Four:	Take a sip and swish the wine around your mouth without gargling.
Tip:	Corked wine tastes sour and vinegary. Don't be afraid to comment if your wine doesn't taste right.
Tip:	If you order the house wine, don't insist on tasting it—if the wine is corked, the restaurant will always replace it.

How to tackle tricky FOODS with GRACE

Canapés

Try to eat a canapé in one bite, so you don't have to deal with it collapsing on you. Decline anything that looks too bulky—an overstuffed mouth is not ladylike. And avoid anything that leaves you with something to hold like a king prawn or chicken skewer.

Olives

Beware of stones; if your olive contains one and there are no receptacles provided for the pits, bring a napkin up to your mouth and discreetly spit the stone into it. Discard the napkin as soon as possible.

Oysters

Give a delicate shake to ensure the oyster has been detached from its shell; otherwise, use an oyster fork to loosen it. Tip the wider end of the shell toward your mouth and keep your head slightly tipped back so the oyster slips smoothly down your throat. Hold the oyster in your mouth for a few seconds to savor the flavor before swallowing whole.

Whole fish

Pull the fish away from the bones with your fork, starting with the fish on the upper side of the spine. Rather than flipping the entire fish over, lift the spine with your knife and scrape out the fish underneath. Don't attack the head or the tail.

Soup

Spoon your soup by scooping away from you, rather than toward you. When trying to reach those last few drops, tip your bowl away from you. Never put your entire spoon in your mouth, don't dip your bread into your soup unless you're in a country where it's expressly encouraged, and never attempt to eat soup when wearing white!

Lobster

Most restaurants serve lobster tails and claws with the shells already cracked open. If they don't, lobster crackers will be provided. Apply pressure slowly so as not to shower other guests in rouge pieces of shell or to damage the meat inside. Once cracked, gently pull the meat out with your fork—it should come freely. You'll find the most meat in the tail, some in the claws, and in the legs sometimes a pink-colored roe. Twist off the legs and delicately suck it out, if you dare!

Sushi

In one hand, hold chopsticks parallel midway down their length. Rest your middle finger between the two sticks and use your thumb and forefinger to hold the top one. Keep the bottom stick still and grip morsels of food with the top one. Put a whole piece of sushi in your mouth rather than biting or trying to break it into pieces. Pour soy sauce onto your plate, rather than directly onto sushi, and eat the pickled ginger separately, as a palate cleanser.

DINNER CONVERSATION

As with any conversation, keep things lively and upbeat at a formal dinner party by asking questions of those around you and by showing interest in the answers. This will lead to deeper conversation and hopefully highlight common interests. If you are finding it difficult to find the common ground, this doesn't have to be a disaster, simply invite more guests into the conversation.

Avoid controversial topics such as money, sex, and politics. And worst of all, avoid unsavory topics that are likely to put other guests off their food. They will not want to hear about your hernia operation or your strict diet while munching on their dessert. Finally, avoid pointing out bad manners; yours may be impeccable but being ladylike also means putting up with people who aren't as refined.

DINING DILEMMAS

Sometimes, all the careful preparation in the world cannot save us from those nightmare scenarios in which a lady's veneer has the potential to crack. Here's how to combat the worst.

YOU HAVE FOOD STUCK BETWEEN YOUR TEETH

If you can sense an offending article in your teeth, the best thing to do is to excuse yourself from the table and remove the dental deviant in the privacy of the bathroom. Never launch an attack while still at the table. If you cannot possibly steal away, bring your napkin to conceal your mouth with one hand and dislodge the food as quickly as possible with the other.

YOU NOTICE SOMEONE ELSE HAS

Discreetly alert your companion to the food by indicating toward your own teeth. Hopefully this is all it will take for them to realize the situation. If not, let them know quietly, without allowing anyone else to hear.

YOU FIND YOURSELF CHEWING ON A PIECE OF GRISTLE

If you don't think a gulp of water will help the sucker slip down, very discreetly bring your napkin to your mouth and spit the gristle into it. Dispose of it as soon as possible.

How best to order in a restaurant

If you are fairly sure your companion is picking up the tab, be respectful and don't opt for the most expensive thing on the menu. If you are dining in a group, decide beforehand how many courses you plan to eat.

To indicate to the waiter that you are ready to make your order, close your menu and place it on the table in front of you. If you are still ignored, politely stay "excuse me" to get the waiter's attention. Never shout, call out, click your fingers, or be aggressive.

Sending food back

Again, a good attitude is the order of the day. Don't shoot the messenger—be polite to the waiter and explain the problem as clearly as possible. They should replace your meal and may even take the cost of it off the total. Remember that this criticism of the meal can cause a bad atmosphere, so think twice about kicking up a fuss when you are in a big group. Sometimes it's just not worth it.

Splitting the bill

Finances and friends don't mix well, so be prepared to pay over the odds if it will make for a more amicable experience. If you know you have eaten more courses or ordered more expensive dishes than your friends, offer to pay more, and if you have to leave early, make a larger contribution than necessary, so no one is left to pick up your tab. If someone offers to pay for you, it's polite to protest once, but then accept graciously. Always tip good service—10-15 percent is usual in the United Kingdom, for example; whereas in the United States, you need to opt for 15-20 percent.

How to be the
perfect hostess

You can always find a reason to host a bash, but before you dive into
your domestic-goddess role, consider the following:

Consider . . .	
The type of celebration	Is this a casual get-together with friends or a huge gathering to celebrate something more significant?
The mix of guests	The guest list is crucial. Combine old friends with new; throw in a few characters and a few listeners.
The venue	Will your sitting room suffice or will you be hiring out a bar for your big bash?
The food and drink	Canapés and cocktails? Afternoon tea? A pizza party? A six-course dinner?
Invitations	These will let your guests know the tone of your event. An e-mail or a text indicates a casual soirée, whereas a professionally printed card received through the mail shows this is a far more chic affair. Ask your guests to RSVP so you have an idea of numbers and don't forget to declare your dress code (and then overdress a little yourself!).

TABLE SETTINGS

For a formal setting, remember that a white linen tablecloth and napkins never go out of fashion, but napkins rings and swan- or lily-shaped napkins do! Keep things simple with white linen and white crockery (food always looks better against a white background). Provide at least one wineglass, a tumbler for water, and a different set of cutlery for every course. Make sure candles and floral arrangements are not so high that they dominate the table and impede conversation.

For a more informal affair, you can be more creative. A low table can be surrounded by cushions for Japanese-style dining, or drag armchairs into the garden for an ultra comfy afternoon tea. Instead of a tablecloth, use stylish wrapping paper as a runner (it's also easier to throw away after the meal). Celebrate your mismatched crockery and cutlery and combine with a few small vases, each filled with a single bloom, to turn them into a feature. No matter how basic your environment, candlelight will make everything look prettier and a bit of imagination is sure to impress your guests.

SERVING DRINKS

Allow for around half a bottle of wine per guest, but always make sure you have extra just in case. It's fine to stick to wine and beer, but it's a nice touch to offer a gin and tonic or even a signature cocktail for the evening (choose something light and fruity and not too alcoholic—you don't want your guests to get sozzled before the food is served). Port is also a classic option to go with a cheese board at the end of the meal. And don't forget soft drinks: keep a supply of fruit juice and sparkling water at the ready.

Stock up on tea and coffee too—both the regular kind and decaffeinated. Avoid instant coffee—a freshly brewed pot smells delicious and is just as easy to make. Have earl grey, green tea, and fruit teas on hand alongside your classic black tea.

REFINED AND EVERYDAY SAMPLE MENUS

No doubt you will have a vast array of recipes to consider when planning the food for your next event. But remember that food does not need to be fussy to be appreciated and even impressive. Consider these menu suggestions and cheat's cooking directions for the sorts of foods appropriate to each occasion:

Something to Impress	
Foie gras	Serve this extra-rich French goose with melba toast.
Salmon en croute	Place a large salmon fillet on a sheet of ready-rolled pastry before baking to make this quick but impressive dish. Whiz rocket and cream cheese in a food processor to make a sauce to serve alongside.
Lemon mousse	For a cheat's version of this impressive dessert, whisk together thickened cream, lemon zest and juice, and superfine sugar to taste before folding through light cream cheese. Refrigerate for at least two hours and serve with berries.

A Weekday Supper

Mushrooms on toast	Warm a selection of different kinds of mushrooms in a pan with garlic, butter, and fresh thyme, then pile on a slice of toasted crusty bread.
Chicken, apricots, and couscous	Serve a warm salad of grilled chicken strips, couscous, toasted pine nuts, chopped dried apricots, and cilantro. One-pot mains such as this one are ideal for a friendly supper.
Caramelized nectarines with vanilla ice-cream	Bake nectarines with a few dabs of butter and a sprinkling of sugar. Serve with good-quality vanilla ice-cream or cream.

The Perfect Hostess Always . . .

✓ Circulates through her guests and makes an effort to have a short conversation with everyone who attends.

✓ Ensures her guests are fed and watered, by handing out nibbles, topping up glasses, or employing someone to do it for her.

✓ Encourages conversation between guests by introducing them to one another and bringing up topics they have in common.

✓ Keeps her cool during spills, kerfuffles, and arguments.

CHAPTER
5

OUT AND ABOUT

In this chapter, you'll learn:

❖ The importance of politeness on public transportation
❖ How to be a good friend ❖ How to maintain your ladylike
composure in other countries ❖ The modern rules of
dating and falling in love ❖ Correspondence
and modern communication

THE LADY IN SOCIETY

While it's all very well for your friends to think of you as charming, gracious, and ladylike, it's no good for those you come across while out and about to encounter a Mr. Hyde side to your character. Allow ladylike manners and style to shine through in everything you do, whether it's traveling on the subway, hailing a cab, or responding to an invitation and you will command respect in all the day-to-day goings-on of your life. If going to another country, a lady always considers the implications of her behavior—what is acceptable at home may not be in all countries—and moderates herself accordingly.

And of course there is romance. As we all know, we will have to kiss quite a few frogs in the search for Mr. Right, and the modern rules and pitfalls of dating don't make the process much easier. If you follow the ladylike guide to love contained in this chapter however, the guys will be falling at your feet in no time!

Consider also how modern technology has demanded a rethink of the old rules of etiquette. The way you send text messages, speak on your cell phone, and write e-mails matters. These can all be done in ways that are either ladylike or unladylike. Read on for an indispensable guide to navigating your way through society, both at home and away.

THE EXPRESS TRAIN TO GOOD MANNERS

Planes, trains, and subways all have one thing in common: other travelers. Buck the modern trend to be lazy and rude when traveling and instead be sensitive to your fellow commuters. Always allow others to step off the train or bus before you enter, only take up one seat (even if this means piling your luggage on top of you), and be quick to give up your seat for pregnant women, those traveling with young children, the elderly, or the less able. If you're feeling chatty, make sure your neighbor is equally keen to talk before diving into conversation—this is especially important on a plane, where your companion really cannot escape.

These might sound like rules drummed into you from childhood, and there's a reason for that—they make for pleasant society and they still apply today.

ON THE ROAD

A lady never allows herself to be overcome by road rage. Keep your wits about you on the road by taking plenty of deep breaths when another driver cuts you off or displays poor manners. Drive as you'd hope everyone else would too—let people out in front of you, never flash your lights at slow drivers, cut in too close behind another car, or make rude hand gestures. Yes, it is possible to be a considerate driver, even if you're in a hurry. Such is the test of a true lady.

Hailing a cab

You will be standing on the street all night if you are shy and retiring when hailing a taxi. Stand confidently at the side of the road and raise your arm to make yourself more visible to cab drivers. Don't whistle or holler. And be fair—if there are people ahead of you hailing cabs, let them take the first one that arrives. If, on the other hand, someone tries to take your taxi, be polite but firm; being a lady does not mean being a pushover. If the situation escalates and threatens to develop into a screaming row, remember that it's more important to keep your cool. Pick your battles and don't allow such encounters to color your day. It's not worth it.

iPod etiquette

There is nothing more annoying than listening to the tinny sound seeping out of someone else's headphones. For this reason, keep your own volume down when on public transportation. There's no reason why a modern lady can't listen to music on headphones. Just remember that it is extremely rude to keep headphones in your ears while communicating with someone else, even if your music is turned off, so pack away your headphones the moment you start a conversation.

Ps and Qs

Whether you are buying a ticket on the bus or are trying to squeeze your way through a crowded street, never forget to be polite. A "please," "thank you," or "excuse me" will ease the way for you and make those around you feel a little bit appreciated too. Do you despair about the lack of basic politeness in general society? Well, make sure you're never part of the problem, and be careful to use these niceties that make daily life so much easier for those around you.

BEING PUNCTUAL

Before cell phones, we seemed to make more effort to be on time, because we had no way of letting our friends know we were running late. Sadly, times have changed. Don't fall prey to tardiness. It creates a bad first impression, which is always difficult to shake off. Being five or ten minutes late is OK; anything more than 15 is not. If you are someone who is constantly late for engagements, consider how you need to change your getting-ready routine to allow more time to get where you need to go.

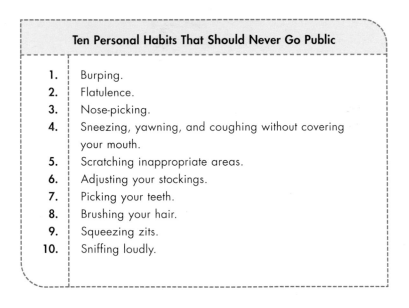

Ten Personal Habits That Should Never Go Public

1. Burping.
2. Flatulence.
3. Nose-picking.
4. Sneezing, yawning, and coughing without covering your mouth.
5. Scratching inappropriate areas.
6. Adjusting your stockings.
7. Picking your teeth.
8. Brushing your hair.
9. Squeezing zits.
10. Sniffing loudly.

The Rules for Being a Good Friend

✓ Phone when you say you will.

✓ Always remember your friend's birthday.

✗ Don't tell their secrets.

✗ Don't be judgmental.

✓ Always be a shoulder to cry on.

✓ Return anything that you borrowed swiftly and in good condition.

✗ Never steal a friend's boyfriend.

✗ Don't gossip about your friend behind their back.

✓ Let her sleep on your sofa if she misses her train, has a fight with her boyfriend, or is too sozzled to drive home.

✗ Don't comment on a friend's weight.

✗ Don't copy a girlfriend's style.

✓ Help her with job applications, moving to a new home, and dinner party preparations.

OPENING DOORS

You know the old rule of etiquette that a man opens a door for a woman? Don't allow your feminist streak to throw the baby out with the bathwater; allow your male companion to offer this mark of respect and enjoy it. If, however, it is a revolving door, wait for the gentleman to enter first. And if you are with another woman, make the move to open the door and allow her to go through before you do.

FOREIGN TRAVEL

Travel to other countries can be an etiquette minefield. There are so many opportunities to offend, be misinterpreted, or simply to misbehave unintentionally. What could be considered the height of bad manners in one country is perfectly acceptable in another. It is perfectly acceptable, for example, to flip a whole fish over when you have finished eating one side in the United States, but is considered bad luck in China.

The best thing to do before any trip is some solid research. Buy a travel guide and learn something of the country's customs. Pay particular attention to tipping suggestions and when in doubt, err on the side of generous. Beware also that in many countries tax for an item is added at the register, so you can expect to pay more than the ticket suggests.

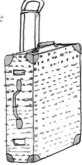

Whichever country you are in, the locals will be friendlier if you make an effort to understand and immerse yourself in their culture. Learn how to say "hello," "goodbye," and "thank you," plus such useful phrases as "how much does it cost?" as well as ways to order food in their language. Sample local dishes and be aware of international dress codes—it may be perfectly acceptable to walk around in hot pants and a bikini top in Brazil, but in Dubai you'll be expected to cover up.

FALLING IN LOVE

A modern lady will be on the lookout for a modern gentleman—someone charming, worldly, and debonair. But there's no need to sit in your turret waiting for your knight in shining armor; you need to seek out the man of your dreams. Being a modern lady does not mean being passive. It's all about the manner in which you catch that fish.

The dating scene can bring its own etiquette hurdles. How do you let a man know you're interested but not easy? How do you turn someone down delicately? And if you are presented with that diamond ring but you hate the setting, how do you say so politely? Read on for a ladylike guide to falling in love...

HOW TO FLIRT

Don't be coy. Flirting is one of the most enjoyable pastimes in the world. But there's a fine line between bold and brash, so you want to make sure you are on the right side of it.

To lure your man, start with a lingering look, hold his gaze for a few seconds longer than normal, and break into a smile. Once you've established your interest, make yourself available for him to approach you—walk past him or linger at the bar, if appropriate. When you start a conversation, make it light and playful. Compliment him—but not too much, you don't want to appear too available. Play it cool and keep him eager with subtle comments instead. It's fine to touch his arm lightly, but don't hold on for too long. Flirting is all about giving a little, but not too much.

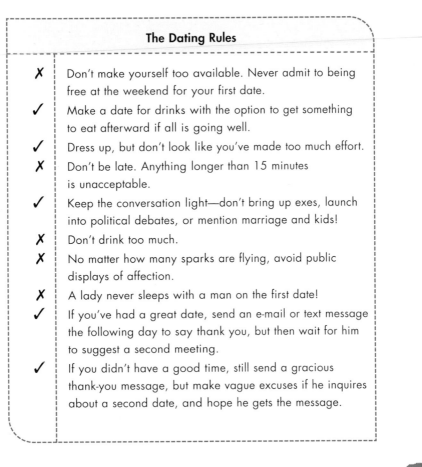

The Dating Rules

✗ Don't make yourself too available. Never admit to being free at the weekend for your first date.

✓ Make a date for drinks with the option to get something to eat afterward if all is going well.

✓ Dress up, but don't look like you've made too much effort.

✗ Don't be late. Anything longer than 15 minutes is unacceptable.

✓ Keep the conversation light—don't bring up exes, launch into political debates, or mention marriage and kids!

✗ Don't drink too much.

✗ No matter how many sparks are flying, avoid public displays of affection.

✗ A lady never sleeps with a man on the first date!

✓ If you've had a great date, send an e-mail or text message the following day to say thank you, but then wait for him to suggest a second meeting.

✓ If you didn't have a good time, still send a gracious thank-you message, but make vague excuses if he inquires about a second date, and hope he gets the message.

TO CALL OR NOT TO CALL?

Calling a man you like is acceptable and admirable in a "taking the bull by the horns" sort of way. E-mailing and texting is even easier because you can say everything you want to without worrying about awkward silences or embarrassed mumblings. Whichever method of communication you choose, the rule is to make contact only once, then wait for him to respond. When he does, wait for a day or two before making your next move.

INVITING HIM HOME . . .

Your first and second dates went well and now on your third meeting you are ready to take things further. Once you invite a man home, you're essentially asking him to stay the night (do people ever really go home after that coffee?). So make sure that's exactly what you want before extending the offer. If intimacy could be the order of the evening, give your pad a quick spruce before heading out—no dirty dishes or laundry visible and you should have both wine and beer in the fridge. When you casually suggest ending the night at your place, you'll both know the subtext of this offer.

. . . IN THE BEDROOM

Until now you have been thoroughly modern, so this isn't the moment to become coy. Let him know what you enjoy—and what you are not comfortable with. Don't be self-conscious: nudity is unavoidable and the right lighting (think lamps or candles) will make it more bearable. Bringing up contraception is essential, but can be a passion killer, so get it out of the way quickly and have condoms close at hand. Sadly, sex doesn't always happen the way it is portrayed in the movies, so keep a sense of humor about you and laugh off any awkward moments or false starts. The following morning, be bright and breezy and always offer breakfast, even if you're not sure you want him to stay.

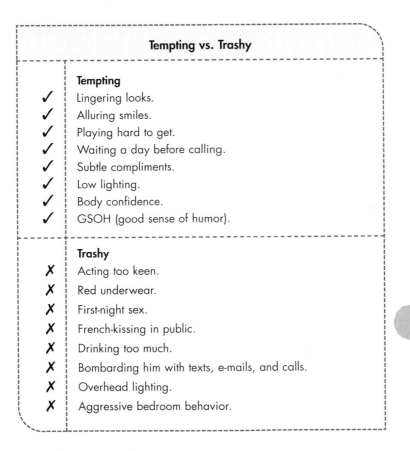

Tempting vs. Trashy

Tempting
✓ Lingering looks.
✓ Alluring smiles.
✓ Playing hard to get.
✓ Waiting a day before calling.
✓ Subtle compliments.
✓ Low lighting.
✓ Body confidence.
✓ GSOH (good sense of humor).

Trashy
✗ Acting too keen.
✗ Red underwear.
✗ First-night sex.
✗ French-kissing in public.
✗ Drinking too much.
✗ Bombarding him with texts, e-mails, and calls.
✗ Overhead lighting.
✗ Aggressive bedroom behavior.

GIFT GIVING

Flowers, chocolates, lingerie, and weekends away are all quite lovely, thank you, but what should you give in return? Gifts can be tricky to negotiate, especially if you haven't been together very long—you don't want him to run a mile when you present him with the keys to a Porsche after two dates!

Never ignore (or forget!) a birthday—if it's early days, a nice meal and a token gift without too much sentimental significance is appropriate. A cult book, his favorite chocolates or sweets, a CD, or DVD of one of his favorite movies are all good choices. Avoid clothing or aftershave until you've been together a while longer. If you can pick up on one of his hobbies and buy a gift accordingly, even better.

Don't splash out on expensive gifts until you've been together for around a year, then the world's your oyster. Think about splurging on that expensive sweater he's been eyeing up, a weekend away, or high-tech gadgets (the male equivalent of a designer bag—you can't go wrong here!).

Whatever you buy, at whatever stage in your relationship, beware of pushing your own tastes on him, so choose clothing, aftershave, artwork, music, and movies that appeal to him, not just to you.

MEETING THE PARENTS

If there's ever been a time to present the very best version of yourself
to those around you, then this is it. Follow these guidelines to win
parental approval:

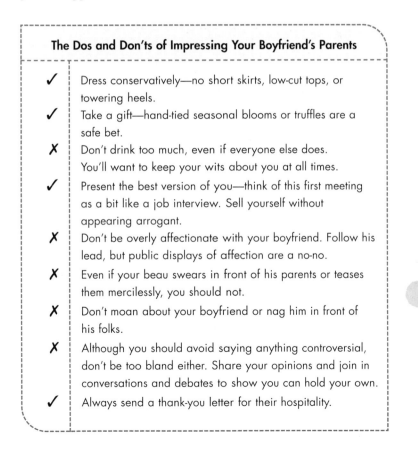

The Dos and Don'ts of Impressing Your Boyfriend's Parents

✓   Dress conservatively—no short skirts, low-cut tops, or towering heels.

✓   Take a gift—hand-tied seasonal blooms or truffles are a safe bet.

✗   Don't drink too much, even if everyone else does. You'll want to keep your wits about you at all times.

✓   Present the best version of you—think of this first meeting as a bit like a job interview. Sell yourself without appearing arrogant.

✗   Don't be overly affectionate with your boyfriend. Follow his lead, but public displays of affection are a no-no.

✗   Even if your beau swears in front of his parents or teases them mercilessly, you should not.

✗   Don't moan about your boyfriend or nag him in front of his folks.

✗   Although you should avoid saying anything controversial, don't be too bland either. Share your opinions and join in conversations and debates to show you can hold your own.

✓   Always send a thank-you letter for their hospitality.

Proposals

Saying yes to a proposal from the man of your dreams is easy. You know it's right if you know it's right; it's what you've hoped for all along.

But don't get caught up in the moment and agree to something you are not 100 percent certain about. Saying no is not quite so simple. Remember that while a marriage proposal might be a complete shock to you, he's probably been dwelling on it for a while. Let him down gently. Tell him how much it means to you but be honest if you do not feel the same way. He does deserve a reason—if you aren't ready yet, but you don't want to break up, you must impress on him how much you love him and want to stay together. A rejected marriage offer can be hard for some men to overcome and his pride may well be dented. If you don't love him enough, it's only fair to let him go, so that he can find a girl who does.

And what if you know that the man you are with is The One but he hasn't popped the question yet and you're getting tired of waiting? The modern lady doesn't wait for the penny to drop. It's perfectly acceptable to seize the opportunity, get down on your bended knee, and to pop the question to the modern gentleman. If he knows you so well, he'll love you for it (and be a little relieved).

What to do if you don't like the ring

This is a tricky one, but no matter how polite you are, no one wants to live with a ring they aren't totally in love with. Give yourself a few days to see if it grows on you, and if it doesn't, tell him gently how you feel and why it's not quite perfect (the diamond not being big enough doesn't count!). Suggest that you'd love to choose the ring together with him. Perhaps suggest a new setting for the gem he's given you.

CORRESPONDENCE

While e-mails, phone calls, and texts are all very well, nothing can compare with the thrill of receiving a handwritten note in the mail. A modern lady knows how to woo and charm with the little extra effort it takes to put pen to paper.

Invest in a set of personalized stationery—white or cream cards on a good-quality stock, engraved or printed with your name and address. These can be used for anything from thank-you cards or smart notes to friends to invitations. Make them even more individual by opting for envelopes with a colored tissue inlay. If this is out of your price range, keep an eye out for packets of chic blank cards that can be used for anything from birthday cards to acceptance notes.

ACCEPTANCE, REGRETS, APOLOGIES, AND **THANK YOUS**

Whether you plan to attend a party, want to send your regrets, or are thanking a host after an event, the most important thing to remember is that time is of the essence. Send your correspondence within two days of receiving an invitation or attending an event. Sending an e-mail is fine, but as always, a handwritten note is more ladylike and will appear more thoughtful.

THE FIRST RULE OF MODERN COMMUNICATION: BE UNAVAILABLE!

With so many electronic gadgets about our person, it's no secret that we can be contacted anywhere at any time. Sadly this means we find it almost impossible to give people our full attention at any time. If at all possible, don't answer work phone calls or e-mails out of work time, don't read texts or take calls in company, never place your phone or beeper on a table during a meal, and if you can possibly switch it off, do!

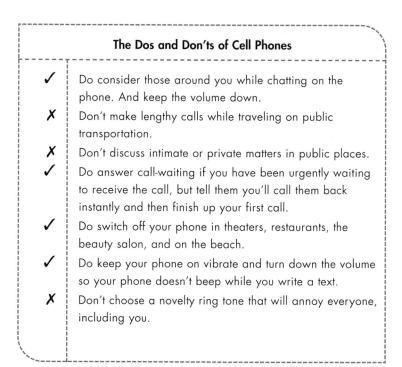

The Dos and Don'ts of Cell Phones

✓ Do consider those around you while chatting on the phone. And keep the volume down.

✗ Don't make lengthy calls while traveling on public transportation.

✗ Don't discuss intimate or private matters in public places.

✓ Do answer call-waiting if you have been urgently waiting to receive the call, but tell them you'll call them back instantly and then finish up your first call.

✓ Do switch off your phone in theaters, restaurants, the beauty salon, and on the beach.

✓ Do keep your phone on vibrate and turn down the volume so your phone doesn't beep while you write a text.

✗ Don't choose a novelty ring tone that will annoy everyone, including you.

NETIQUETTE

E-mail has become such an integral part of our daily lives it's almost impossible to imagine we lived without it. It might have revolutionized the way we communicate but if you ignore good e-mail etiquette, your friends, family, and colleagues will bemoan your poor netiquette. Consider the following guidelines.

Don't ramble in e-mails. It is still more civilized to speak to a friend if you have something to say, and nothing can beat hearing the voice of someone you care about. Stick to the point and only write about things that matter. Don't bombard everyone in your e-mail address book with bad jokes and chain e-mails.

Finally, and most importantly, remember that e-mails cannot express a tone of voice like speaking can, so think about how your e-mail could be interpreted before sending it. Never send personal e-mails through your work account and never send e-mails when you are angry—a nasty e-mail cannot be withdrawn once you have hit the send button.

CHAPTER
6

NINE TO FIVE

In this chapter, you'll learn:

❖ How to get the job ❖ Office etiquette
❖ Presentation skills ❖ What to wear to the office
❖ How to cope with your colleagues
❖ International business etiquette

THE SECRET TO YOUR SUCCESS

It may be easy to flex your etiquette skills while sipping Earl Grey from a bone china teacup, but when you're blinking at a computer screen during a ten-hour day behind a desk piled high with work, harried by your colleagues, and with a tight deadline to meet, is it so easy? The modern lady has to deal with the commercial world in a way that the majority of her historical counterparts did not, which makes her quest that much more tricky to negotiate. With that in mind, how do you retain your charm and poise from job interview through to managing your staff?

Being a lady in business means learning how to get ahead fairly and gracefully, and knowing what not to do in a work environment. Keep your head and maintain your poise at all times, and you're halfway there. Avoid the pitfalls of the workplace and you're on your way to a successful career. The skills you have learned so far in this guide are easily translatable to the business world and using them could be the secret to success.

The job interview

You've spied your dream job, but how do you make it yours? The interview is your big chance to sell yourself. Just like meeting your boyfriend's parents for the first time, you need to make the absolute best impression possible.

Start with your outfit. Remind yourself of the golden rules of dressing for an interview (see Chapter 3, page 62). Avoid anything too racy or avant-garde and always opt for more rather than less formal.

Do your homework before your interview. Read up on the company and focus on the specific job for which you're being interviewed. Undoubtedly you will be asked what you can bring to the role, so think about why your skills are suitable and what unique qualities you offer. Even if you're not sure it's the right job for you, be sure to express enthusiasm and sell yourself as best you can during the interview—you might have a different opinion later. You want to be in a position to choose whether or not to take the job and for that you need to convince the employer to offer it to you. If you have been asked to do some work in advance for the interview, always do more than has been requested—there's no such thing as appearing too keen.

In the interview, sit up straight, make eye contact, and smile a lot. Keep in mind the importance of what your body language says about your attitude (see Chapter 2, page 40). Think before speaking, try not to ramble, mumble, or gabble—take a deep breath to slow yourself down and to calm your nerves.

After your meeting, send a follow-up e-mail to thank the employer for their time. It's fine to ask when a decision might be made on who will be hired. If you haven't heard anything three days after this date, you can send an e-mail to inquire about whether a decision has been reached. Good luck!

THE ETIQUETTE OF OFFICE CHITCHAT

Certain topics of conversation are appropriate to share in the office: your new house or the fact that you've just joined a gym, the fact that your birthday is coming up, which is always a good way to maximize on your present haul. You probably see your coworkers every day so naturally they will become more like friends as you share the day-to-day goings-on of life. But intimate details about your love life, your recent argument with your boyfriend, and financial or health issues should be kept to yourself.

If you are looking for another job, you should keep it quiet unless you really trust the person—even though a lady would never betray a person's trust, not everyone's morals are as untarnished as hers. Consider the implications of everything you say before you say it—it might come back at you when you least expect it.

Finally, while you can spend hours discussing your love life over a bottle of wine with your girlfriends, this is not what you are being paid to do in the office (not even the office kitchen), so keep personal conversations brief. If you have made close friends with a colleague and must chat in a personal way, arrange to have that heart-to-heart during your lunch break or after work over a drink— keep it separate from your work time.

GIVING THE PERFECT PRESENTATION

Speaking in front of a room of people isn't easy, but the best way to build your confidence is with practice—the more often you do it, the easier it will become.

Write bullet points for yourself on index cards. Although you don't want to read your entire presentation off cue cards because it will sound too stilted, having jumping-off points will rescue you when you become tongue-tied. Depending on the subject and formality of the presentation, you might want to prepare a digital presentation featuring these bullet points and relevant images, so your audience can read them and view the accompanying material while you are speaking, which will consolidate and reinforce your message. Whatever you have to say, speak clearly and slowly, concentrate on taking a slow breath between sentences so you don't fall over your words, and use the time to catch people's eyes, to make your audience feel included.

The most crucial thing to remember is to be concise. Most people switch off after a couple of minutes, so keep it brief and you'll hold your audience's attention. Decide what you want to say and then edit it back to core statements.

Be confident in what you're saying and speak a bit louder than you think you should, to ensure everyone can hear you. And if you can throw in a little self-deprecating joke, even better—a lady who can laugh at herself, especially in public, shows she is both charming and self-assured. A dash of humor is always a crowd pleaser.

Office phone etiquette

It should go without saying that the office is not the place to be making lengthy personal calls, but this is such an often-flouted rule that it must be emphasized time and again. Save that weekly catch-up with your mother for after-hours. If you do need to make a personal call, be quick and discreet.

When it comes to office phone conversations, check your volume control. The rest of the office doesn't want to listen in to every call. In an open-plan environment there's nothing more distracting than a coworker without the ability to moderate their volume.

And if there's one rule of office etiquette that will stand you in good stead, remember always to return missed work calls. It's easy to get caught up in what you're doing and to forget, but out of courtesy alone you should always try to get back to people promptly.

Online etiquette

Just as it's frowned upon to use the work phone for your personal calls, consider how you use the Internet and your work e-mail. As tempting as it is, don't use your work e-mail for personal messages. Any e-mails of a sensitive nature, or anything that you don't want your IT department to read (which includes anything your company might use against you), should be send via webmail rather than your office e-mail account. However, it's also not good protocol to be checking your webmail hourly, so keep it to a minimum or leave it till you get home.

WHAT TO WEAR TO THE OFFICE

This isn't the place to show off your quirky dress sense—or your killer body. No miniskirts, shorts, four-inch heels, or low-cut tops. A lady's wardrobe may contain all these items but her secret is knowing when and when not to wear them. No one will consider you more professional if you wear risqué clothing and you are running the risk of offending your colleagues or even receiving a disciplinary warning. Piercings and purple hair probably aren't  going to win over your boss (unless he's a punk too!), so while it may seem a little dull, tone down your look during office hours. Want to flaunt your fashionista status? Do it with a designer bag, beautiful shoes, and a vintage Pucci scarf.

Five Things to Remember When it Comes to Elevators

1. If it's very cramped, wait for the next elevator. No one wants their personal space invaded.
2. Let people out before getting in.
3. Don't hold a loud conversation for everyone else to hear.
4. Practice perfect personal hygiene—beware of bad breath, body odour or, worst of all, flatulence!
5. Press the button for only the floor you want to get off at.

HOW TO HAVE A SUCCESSFUL BUSINESS LUNCH

A lunch on the expense account is not a chance to order the lobster and get tipsy on someone else's dime, but it is a great opportunity for you to flex some of your ladylike charm. Before ordering, confer with your companions to decide how many courses you will have. If you are taking someone for lunch, let them order, and then follow their lead—if they opt for a glass of wine, you may too, but if they decide against it, you should also refrain.

Try to sandwich your business talk between small talk at the beginning and end of the lunch, and remember this is a professional environment so steer clear of any topics too personal or racy.

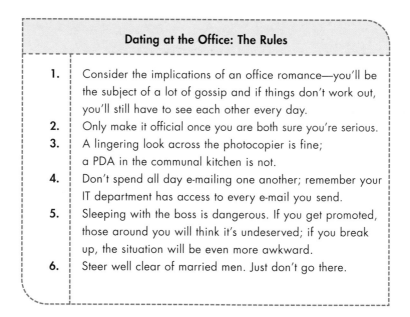

Dating at the Office: The Rules

1. Consider the implications of an office romance—you'll be the subject of a lot of gossip and if things don't work out, you'll still have to see each other every day.
2. Only make it official once you are both sure you're serious.
3. A lingering look across the photocopier is fine; a PDA in the communal kitchen is not.
4. Don't spend all day e-mailing one another; remember your IT department has access to every e-mail you send.
5. Sleeping with the boss is dangerous. If you get promoted, those around you will think it's undeserved; if you break up, the situation will be even more awkward.
6. Steer well clear of married men. Just don't go there.

HOW TO COPE WITH YOUR COLLEAGUES

Colleagues can be a tricky breed, but the modern lady knows that it makes most sense to get along with them best she can, as the office is where she spends the majority of her waking life!

YOUR BOSS

Building a good relationship with your boss might be a challenge, but it's one definitely worth taking, as the rewards can be huge. Even if you are suffering under a difficult manager, it is possible to keep your cool and be ladylike.

Be friendly and courteous at all times—aim to make your boss's life easier by making an extra cup of coffee when you make your own or offering to pick up a sandwich at lunchtime. Don't stray into suck-up territory—weekly bouquets and a flurry of compliments will make you look like a creep. A lady has the confidence to be herself, as well as the humility to know her place and to defer to her boss in the appropriate situations.

Learn the power of "yes"—no boss wants to hear why things have not or cannot be done, and being an effective problem-solver will make you indispensable. To help yourself get ahead, talk to your boss about what you need to achieve to be considered for promotion. In many companies you won't get if you don't ask, so being driven and discussing your desire to move up in the company shows that you are ambitious and assertive.

Your staff

A ladylike boss knows how to manage those beneath her as she would like to be managed herself. This is not the time to go all *Devil Wears Prada*, no matter how one has been treated in the past. As the boss it is your role to encourage your staff to grow and to develop within the company. Don't be threatened by driven employees, but teach them the value of learning to walk before they try to run.

The most important balance here is remembering that you are a boss first and a friend second. You want to be approachable, but need to keep a distance so that if in the uncomfortable event you have to let go of an employee, it's not like you're ditching a friend. Don't forget, bosses should always buy the first round of after-work drinks.

The Dos and Don'ts of Getting Ahead

✓ Do keep an eye on other jobs that may be available—interviews can be good practice.

✓ Do let your boss know your career aspirations and have regular progress meetings.

✓ Do take on more responsibilities than are covered by your job description—but make sure they are noted.

✗ Don't trample on your colleagues to further your career.

✓ Do build a good relationship with your boss.

✓ Do be friendly with everyone in your office to develop a good reputation—you never know where your colleagues will end up.

✗ Don't leave a company on a bad note—it's never worth burning bridges in business.

INTERNATIONAL BUSINESS ETIQUETTE

Think about traveling for business as a form of international diplomacy. To be just as ladylike abroad as you are at home, you need to be educated about the country's culture and customs. Women are perceived very differently in different continents and learning to embrace these differences will help you to be more accepted.

As a general rule, follow the lead of your hosts. Keep an open mind when it comes to dining—while you can politely decline those monkey brains, sampling them could secure you the deal and might well be worth it. Study the most important customs of the country before you visit. In the meantime, here are some key pointers:

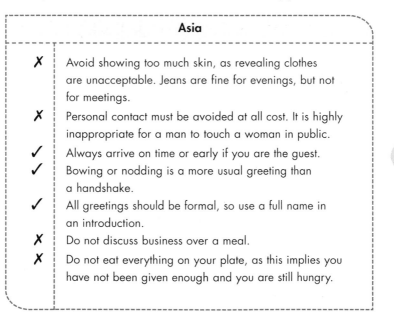

Asia

✗	Avoid showing too much skin, as revealing clothes are unacceptable. Jeans are fine for evenings, but not for meetings.
✗	Personal contact must be avoided at all cost. It is highly inappropriate for a man to touch a woman in public.
✓	Always arrive on time or early if you are the guest.
✓	Bowing or nodding is a more usual greeting than a handshake.
✓	All greetings should be formal, so use a full name in an introduction.
✗	Do not discuss business over a meal.
✗	Do not eat everything on your plate, as this implies you have not been given enough and you are still hungry.

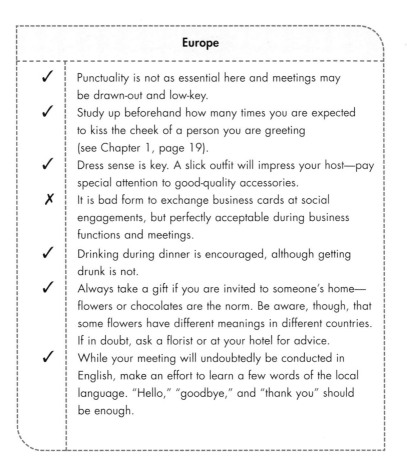

Europe

✓ Punctuality is not as essential here and meetings may be drawn-out and low-key.

✓ Study up beforehand how many times you are expected to kiss the cheek of a person you are greeting (see Chapter 1, page 19).

✓ Dress sense is key. A slick outfit will impress your host—pay special attention to good-quality accessories.

✗ It is bad form to exchange business cards at social engagements, but perfectly acceptable during business functions and meetings.

✓ Drinking during dinner is encouraged, although getting drunk is not.

✓ Always take a gift if you are invited to someone's home— flowers or chocolates are the norm. Be aware, though, that some flowers have different meanings in different countries. If in doubt, ask a florist or at your hotel for advice.

✓ While your meeting will undoubtedly be conducted in English, make an effort to learn a few words of the local language. "Hello," "goodbye," and "thank you" should be enough.

Latin America

✓ While sexy styles of dress may be beach-worthy, stick to dark suits and white shirts for business meetings.

✓ Always maintain eye contact.

✗ Eating on the street or on public transport is considered extremely rude.

✓ Titles are very important—always address a person by their professional title only, such as "professor" for teacher or "abogado" for lawyer (in Spanish-speaking countries).

✓ Good relationships will help shorten what can otherwise become lengthy negotiations. Work hard to build a relationship before you even start doing business.

✓ Be punctual but expect to wait up to 30 minutes for your counterpart.

✓ Touching each other's arms or pats on the back are recognized signs of friendship.

Middle East

✓ | Women must keep their upper arms, chest, back, and legs covered at all times, and wear long pants while exercising.

✗ | Try not to use the word "no," which can offend. Evasive refusals are more appropriate. Never refuse an invitation outright; instead, refer to a clash of engagements.

✗ | Do not thank your host at the end of a meal, as this is considered a form of payment and is therefore insulting.

✓ | It is common to remove your shoes before entering a building—follow the lead of your host.

✗ | Bear in mind that alcohol and pork are illegal in Saudi Arabia.

✗ | Friday is the day of rest for Muslims, so do not arrange a business meeting on this day.

✗ | The left hand is considered unclean, so do not shake hands or eat with it.

✗ | Try not to cross your legs when sitting and never show the bottom of your feet, as these are considered disrespectful.

✗ | The thumbs-up gesture is offensive. Use it at your peril.

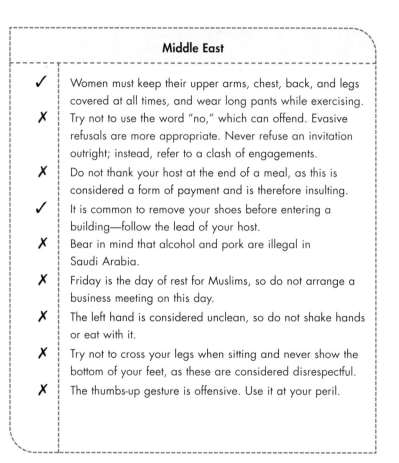

CONCLUSION

Phew! There's a lot to learn, isn't there? But no one said that being a woman of charm, manners, and style was easy. As the practice of good manners and refinement dies out and bad manners become more acceptable, you have the opportunity to stand out as one in a million. Are you willing to be a lady?

Treat people with respect—even those you are squished between on the commuter train, or the grumpy sales assistant who refuses to refund your damaged dress. Go above and beyond to be a good friend—remember birthdays, forgive tantrums, and help clean up after house parties. Be the kind of person that others aspire to imitate, thanks to your impeccable dress sense and effortless manners. Study the lessons contained in this little volume so that when you're in a sticky situation you will know the right thing to say or do.

But remember that modern manners are always evolving, so what might be appropriate now could change quickly and new rules may appear. Take all this in your stride and be prepared to move with the times (while remembering that hot pants and heels will never be a classy look!). Grow old gracefully without forsaking the principles of proper behavior. While your shoes and table setting might go out of style, being a lady never will.

INDEX